M000314498

What's Good About Anger?

Dealing with Rage

Fifth Edition

Foreword by Dr. Rich Pfeiffer

by
Lynette J. Hoy, NCC, LCPC, National Certified Counselor,
Licensed Clinical Professional Counselor,
Anger Management Specialist-V
and
Ted Griffin, Editor/Writer

A CounselCare Connection Publication
Oak Brook, Illinois
www.counselcareconnection.org

May be purchased at the
Anger Management Institute shopping mall:
www.whatsgoodaboutanger.com

What's Good About Anger?
Dealing With Rage
FIFTH EDITION

Requests for information should be addressed to:
CounselCare Connection, P.C.
1200 Harger Rd., Suite 602
Oak Brook, Illinois, 60523
Original printing, 2002. Second edition, 2006.
Third edition, 2012. Fourth Edition, 2016.
ISBN 978-0-578-25269-8

CounselCare Connection Publications
Oak Brook, Illinois
Printed in the United States of America

To my lovely wife Lois, for her gracious patience and persevering love, without which I might never have chosen to allow God to bring my anger under his control.
   Ted Griffin

To my husband, David, who has inspired and encouraged me and demonstrated God's love to me for over 51 years.
   Lynette J. Hoy

Contents

FOREWORD

by Richard Pfeiffer, MDiv, PhD

Whats Good About Anger? keeps getting better and better. It has always been about the transformation of destructive anger into something much more positive. With the addition of a new Emotional Intelligence chapter it has become even more helpful to those of us who suffer from never having been exposed to a healthy way to approach our angry emotions.

Suffering from anger management problems can frequently be a very discouraging plight. For example, one of the difficulties with mismanaged anger is that there is always something that triggers it. But when we are ineffective in managing our anger, we become the unacceptable focus of disdain, and the issue that generated it all often gets lost. It can sometimes seem rather hopeless. How can we move from a psychic reaction that is seemingly life-robbing and destructive to a method of responding to our feelings of anger that is more life-giving?

Lynette Hoy and Ted Griffin have created an anger management program that places an emphasis on hope. The What's Good About Anger? program successfully shifts the hopeless approach focusing on experiences and expressions of anger as "bad," to a method that says "let's learn how to use the benefits of anger for productive purposes." So it is the modeling of an empathic approach to anger problems that allows participants to actually experience "empathy" and find new hope to grow and to develop higher levels of consciousness.

This new edition offers practical solutions to anger problems in the form of helpful skills, concepts, and techniques to help anyone deal with anger more effectively. The program increases awareness of emotions and discusses emotional intelligence in a positive way. The co-authors have touched all the bases of state-of-the-art anger management solutions, doing so in both a scientific and spiritually sensitive manner.

You are in good hands here, and as you take this program seriously you will find the benefits of decreased stress, shame, distorted thinking, and also a lessening of anger itself. You will discover the hope that you have "a moment" to make a choice between either destructive "punishing" or creative problem-solving. We can grow! We can develop to higher levels of consciousness.

Rich Pfeiffer, Author

Richard Pfeiffer, MDiv, PhD, is the President of the Board of Directors for NAMA, the National Anger Management Association: www.namass. org, the Director/Founder of Growth Central, and the author of eight Real Solution Workbooks.

INTRODUCTION AND INSTRUCTIONS
Welcome to the fifth edition
of What's Good About Anger?

It's hard to believe that there is anything good about anger, isn't it? As you read this book, we are hoping that you will discover, though, that you can learn to control your anger and use your anger for good purposes, with the help of your Higher Power.

You can learn how to be good and angry. You can learn how to deal with rage.

What's new in this edition? You will find more in-depth information on triggers for anger, the physiology of anger; key strategies for redirecting anger, application questions geared to help you develop your emotional intelligence; and practical steps on forgiveness and how to apologize.

This fifth edition is about getting the most out of your anger! The book will teach you how to transform your anger into healthy skills for living so you can achieve the goals that you really want in life.

This course emphasizes the source of anger, triggers that provoke anger, and examples of how to express anger through problem- solving, assertiveness, behavioral skills, stress and conflict management, empathy, and forgiveness.

What's Good About Anger? is meant to assist people with differing experiences in all walks of life. People with "hidden" anger who might be feeling depressed. People dealing with explosive anger and rage. Even people who don't believe they have ever felt angry.

So take your time reading through this book and completing the questions and activities. We hope you will come to realize that anger can be a healthy emotion to motivate you to reach your goals in life and relationships.

INSTRUCTIONS FOR USE OF THE WHAT'S GOOD

ABOUT ANGER? DEALING WITH RAGE

1. Complete the Anger Survey. This will help you assess when, where and how you get angry and your general provocation scenario (GPS). The GPS describes typical situations in which you are triggered to become angry. Be honest about your feelings and experience with anger. After all, this course-work is personal and is geared to help you get an understanding of how you can grow in tackling any problem you may be having with anger in your life and in your relationships. The survey and first chapters help you develop "self-awareness" the foundation of emotional intelligence!

2. Then read through the book, completing the questions as you progress. Apply your general provocation scenario (found in the Anger Survey) to the section in the course on "Handling Anger Effectively." Many chapters teach skills to help you grow in "self-management" the second level of emotional intelligence!

3. Keep a weekly anger log and progress report throughout the time you are reading this book. Apply the steps in "Handling Anger Effectively" to each situation.

4. Read "When to Take a Break" in order to make a plan for the situations that come up that cause your anger to escalate more quickly and make you feel like you are losing control. If you still find your anger escalating, then lengthen your time-out period.

5. Read and apply the communication skills taught in the assertiveness and managing conflict chapters. Complete the empathy and assertiveness inventories.

6. Evaluate your thinking with the cognitive distortions questions, and log your thinking patterns. This exercise will help you identify any false perspective you have about people or situations and challenge whether it is correct.

7. Read the chapter on emotional intelligence, rate your level of empathy, and begin applying these important concepts. You will discover how growing in emotional intelligence is essential for redirecting anger into productive behaviors!

8. Read the Rage chapter and take the inventory. If you are experiencing explosive anger – consider getting an evaluation and counseling. Learning and applying the key strategies in the book such as: taking a break, identifying triggers, relaxation strategies and changing your thinking will help you develop control over incidents of rage.

9. Finally complete the chapter "Plan to Change Your Life by Changing Your Thinking," and read the FAQs at the end of the book.

Additional aspects of this course will teach you to apply forgiveness, assertiveness, self-empowerment, problem-solving, empathy, stress and conflict management skills, and foundational principles in order to put your anger to work for good.

GROUP GUIDELINES

The following material will help you if you are part of a group using this book (though it can be used individually).

Individual preparation: Spend time reading each chapter prior to each meeting and answering the questions. Complete any assignments.

Group rules for participation:

1. Keep whatever is said in the group confidential.

2. Use "I" messages vs. "you" messages.

3. Don't give advice unless it is requested.

4. You don't have to talk if you prefer not to.

5. Avoid covering your pain with humor.

Leader guidelines:

1. Ask the participants to agree to keep confidential what is discussed in the group. This will make the group a safe place for sharing and accountability.

2. Promote participation by drawing out quieter people and setting boundaries with those who tend to monopolize.

3. Open the first session by reading the foreword, introduction, and guidelines. Ask people to share what brought them to the group

and what they hope to learn. Direct participants to complete the Anger Survey or part of it—depending on time.

4.   Begin subsequent sessions with a review of the previous week's material. Summarize or read the chapter you are covering, and lead a discussion of the questions. Share your own situations and feelings to provide a role model for group members.

5.   Explore how to apply the coping skills, principles, and new concepts to specific situations people share. Ask: How can you personally apply this principle, technique, or concept to one of your situations/triggers this week?

6.   Conclude each session by discussing the questions provided. Then review any upcoming assignments.

7.   As a group facilitator be aware of the responsibility to report to authorities/family any revelation that indicates someone intends to harm himself or herself or others. Encourage that person to get professional counseling immediately.

1
ANGER SURVEY AND PROGRESS REPORT

P lease answer the following questions as accurately and as completely as possible.

1. How often do you get angry? (Circle one that applies)

(a) daily.

(b) many times a day.

(c) a few times a month.

(d) several times a week.

(e) very rarely.

2. What happens when you get angry? (Circle all that apply):
I tend to:

(a) feel tense.

(b) withdraw.

(c) exercise.

(d) feel sick.

(e) overeat.

(f) distract myself.

(g) tell someone.

(h) raise my voice.

(i) hit someone or something.

(j) become cynical or sarcastic.

(k) take a time-out.

(l) think about how to get even.

(m) avoid the issue.

(n) make light of things or joke about it.

(o) pray.

(p) go out drinking.

(q) argue.

(r) talk it over.

(s) swear.

(t) feel depressed.

(u) other _____ .

Rate the severity of your anger above:

Question 1:

(a) 4

(b) 5

(c) 2

(d) 3

(e) 1

Question 2:

(a) 1	(l) 4
(b) 3	(m) 3
(c) 1	(n) 3
(d) 3	(o) 0
(e) 3	(p) 5
(f) 1	(q) 4
(g) 1	(r) 1
(h) 4	(s) 4
(i) 5	(t) 4
(j) 4	(u) 3 (if a negative or harmful response)
(k) 1	

Total your scores from questions 1 and 2 together.

Assess the category you are in:

Category I: 1-10 points = little problem with anger.
Category II: 10-20 points = moderate problem with anger.

* If either Category I or II includes trouble with the law, injury to others or self, drinking, depression, outbursts, experiencing anger several times a day, etc. then you have a serious problem with anger—Category III.

Category III: 20 points and above = serious problem with anger.

3. Which people tend to trigger your anger?
(check all that apply):

☐ significant others.

☐ co-workers.

☐ policemen.

☐ boss.

☐ friends.

☐ strangers.

☐ men.

☐ women.

☐ others: _____ .

4. What situations or behavior tend to trigger your anger?

(check all that apply):

When people:

☐ treat me unfairly.

☐ disrespect me.

☐ ignore me.

☐ put me down.

☐ threaten me.

☐ interrupt me.

☐ keep me waiting.

☐ joke about me.

☐ hit me.

☐ other: _____ .

When I am:

☐ working.

☐ disappointed with someone.

☐ missing someone.

☐ experiencing loss or change.

☐ under stress.

☐ late to events.

☐ unable to achieve my goals.

☐ unable to share my opinions.

☐ bored.

☐ in a crisis.

☐ other: _____ .

Write out a recent situation when you felt angry:

What happened?

Where was it?

How long did you feel angry?

With whom were you angry?

How did you react?

5. Where are you most likely to get angry?

(check all that apply):

☐ at home.

☐ at work.

☐ in social situations.

☐ during sports or recreation activities.

☐ driving.

☐ in public.

☐ other: _____ .

6. What happens after you get angry?

(Circle all that apply):

(a) someone gets hurt.

(b) I feel guilty.

(c) my relationships are disrupted.

(d) I feel defensive.

(e) I get in trouble with the law.

(f) I try to make restitution or reconcile with the person.

(g) I ask God for wisdom and guidance.

(h) I don't talk to the other person.

(i) I can't stop thinking about the event/person.

(j) I get depressed or think about harming myself.

(k) I lose sleep or can't eat.

(l) I feel relieved.

(m) I have been asked to leave.

(n) I get in trouble at work.

(o) others say I have a problem with anger.

(p) I want to run away.

(q) other: _____ .

Rate your answers from question 6 above.

___ You handle anger pretty well if you checked only b, f, g and l. Anger is not disrupting your life, but you could be dealing with hidden anger.

___ You are unable to control your anger and your anger is causing serious interference in your life and relationships if you checked any of these: a, c, e, h, i, j, k, m, n, o, p, q (if "other" is an unhealthy response).

7. How do you normally help yourself calm down when you feel angry? (check all that apply):

☐ deep breathing and relaxation techniques.

☐ prayer.

☐ counting to ten.

☐ reading inspirational books like the Bible.

☐ telling myself: "This is not worth getting angry over."

☐ thinking about the negative consequences that could result from getting angry and losing control.

☐ thinking about what the real issue is.

I tell myself:

☐ "This person is not making sense now. He/she may have had a bad day."

☐ "I'm going to try to work through this problem reasonably."

☐ "I should try to cooperate—he's/she's making sense."

☐ "Maybe I should take a time-out until I cool down."

☐ "I should try to understand what this person is upset about by listening and paraphrasing."

Other things you say or do to control yourself or the situation (positive or negative):

_____ .

_____ .

_____ .

_____ .

_____ .

_____ .

General Provocation Scenario: In the space below, write out a typical situation in which you find yourself getting annoyed or angry. Pretend it is a play. Describe what happened, who was involved, when and where it happened, and what transpired beforehand. Then write out what each person said and did including your thoughts, communication, and behavior.

Who:

Where:

When:

What led up to this scene:

The scene opens:

What I think: What I do:

What I say:

What the other person says/does:

How did you recently control or not control your anger?

Write out:

What happened?

What triggered your angry response?

What were the circumstances?

What were your thoughts?

What were you telling yourself?

Who else was involved?

Evaluate your angry response using the steps from the Handling Anger Effectively chapter, and apply your situations to the model given.

Log Your Anger:

Write down the situations when you get angry, and rate them:

1. When did you last feel angry?

2. What happened and with whom?

3. What were you thinking when this occurred?

Example: "He/she never understands." "I am just a failure." "I can't handle this." "He/she doesn't care about me." "This situation is hopeless." "I will never succeed." "That person meant to ignore me." "This project is dead in the water." "I couldn't have done a worse job." "That person never should have cut me off." "If I had just prayed more, I never would have lost my job." "He's such a loser." You get the idea.

4. Rate the strength of the anger:

1 = lowest; 5 = moderate; 10 = strongest.

1   2   3   4   5   6   7   8   9   10

5. Continue to keep a log for one to two weeks, then evaluate your angry responses as suggested below.

What could you have changed?

Did you take any time-outs to cool down?

Evaluate your angry response:

How did it affect you and others?

Was it destructive; did it lead to resentment and

broken relationships?

Did it lead to problem-solving, restoring relationships,

and honest (loving) dialogue?

Did you seek spiritual help or counsel?

What would help you control your anger in the future?

What was your thinking prior to and during the episode of anger? Do you have any of the Cognitive Distortions found in the book?

Now go to "Handling Anger Effectively," and apply your situations to the model given.

ANGER MANAGEMENT PROGRESS REPORT:*

Week _____ :

1.   Anger Survey results (circle one):

Category I   Category II   Category III

2.   Identify triggers:

3.   Identify present coping skill use:

Please measure your use of anger coping skills from 1-10: _____

(1 = poor use of skills; 5 = intermittent use of skills; 10 = consistent use of skills)

4. How is your anger presently affecting:

Work:	greatly	moderately	little	none
Marriage:	greatly	moderately	little	none

Family:	greatly	moderately	little	none
Friends:	greatly	moderately	little	none
School:	greatly	moderately	little	none
Legal:	greatly	moderately	little	none
Personal:	greatly	moderately	little	none
Goals:	greatly	moderately	little	none
Other:	greatly	moderately	little	none

(describe other: _____)

5. Describe one angry or frustrated episode/situation from this past week:

What happened and with whom?

What triggered your anger?

What were your thoughts?

How did you respond?

What skill did you try to use?

Was it effective?

Underline the following coping skills from the book that you could implement in the future:

• time-out

• assertiveness

- problem-solving

- let it go

- change thinking

- forgive

- pray

- conflict management skills

- avoid triggers, etc.

How have you improved?

* Course participants are granted permission to copy the Anger Management Progress Report weekly for personal use only.

2
ANGER'S
MANY FACES

Anger, though potentially harmful, can be transformed into a positive force accomplishing great good in our lives.
Ted Griffin and Lynette Hoy

Lynette's Story

I can remember the day one of my sisters came home with a suspension slip for throwing an orange in the lunchroom. My father dragged her upstairs to the attic. There were loud noises, yelling, and crying. She limped down the stairs, bloody and bruised.

I can remember the beatings in the basement with a board, my father's rage, the pain and the fear.

I can remember experiencing a "cold shoulder" for days when I would disappoint someone in my family.

I can remember my husband and I up in the attic of our second-story rented flat, two weeks after our daughter was born, screaming at each other and throwing things. I don't remember what caused the anger or why it hurt so much. But I experienced anger's pain, inner wounds, and loneliness.I learned that anger was something to be feared, that it was cruel, loud, cold, silent, resentful, and threatening.

Ted's Story

I have long feared anger—my father's and my own. My dad, an alcoholic who's drinking kept him from connecting with his family, had a quiet anger. He didn't beat us or yell at us for hours—he just sort of ignored us. My anger—which was really years' worth of bitterness toward Dad—became violent, abusive and dangerous, especially after my father died and I couldn't express my anger to the one I was really mad at because he wasn't around anymore.

Looking back, I am ashamed of many of the things I said and did at that stage of my life. And I thank God for helping me forgive my father and learn how to be kind to my family—a family I almost lost because of my rage. Not all anger is wrong, but when it's like mine was, only God can keep the individual and his family from going over the cliff. The journey hasn't been easy or quick, but God has sustained me every step of the way, and He continues to do so. Not everyone turns to faith to deal with their anger, but that is what made the difference in my life.

All of us have experienced anger. Some of us have cringed under the rage in our families, struggled with it in our souls, felt it toward our friends and loved ones. Some of us have shocked others with volcanoes of anger.

But anger is not just a personal enemy. The evidence abounds that we live in a mad, mad, mad world. Statistics from American Demographics tell us:

- 23% of Americans admit they openly express their anger.

- 39% say they hold it in or hide it.

- 23% say they walk away from the situation.

- 23% confess to having hit someone in anger.

- 17% admit they have destroyed the property of someone who made them mad.

We want to demonstrate to you that anger, though potentially harmful, is a complex emotion we can come to understand and a positive force that can accomplish great good in our lives.

What Is Anger?

When you think about anger, what words or pictures come to mind? Frustration? Rage? Anger can be defined as an aversive state ranging from annoyance to rage. Webster's says, "Anger is a strong feeling of displeasure and antagonism, indignation or an automatic reaction to any real or imagined insult, frustration, or injustice, producing emotional agitation seeking expression."

Let's look at the problem of anger in our society. Anger's effects are evident. There is rampant violence in schools, families, and neighborhoods. For example:

- Severe violence is a chronic feature of 13% of all marriages and generally 35 violent incidents occur before any type of report is made.

- Every twenty-five seconds someone is a victim of a violent crime such as murder, robbery, assault, or rape.

- Nearly a million children are abused by their parents annually.

- Adolescents represent 12% of the population but account for 39% of all violent crime.

(Gintner, p. 2.)

Anger is one of the most troubling emotions! We sometimes hear blatant admonishments such as "we shouldn't ever be angry." So what happens to our anger? We end up feeling guilty for being angry, or we pretend we're not angry, or we numb our feelings or turn our anger into depression.

How do you feel when you're driving down the expressway and someone cuts in front of you, almost causing an accident? Or your mother tells you, "You'll never change—you should be more like your sister/brother?" Or your boss blames you for something you didn't do? What kinds of emotions do you feel then? Frustration and anger are normal responses to these situations. But sometimes we not only have difficulty owning up to and honestly expressing our anger, but then we feel worse because of the guilt that ensues as a result of feeling angry.

Foundational Insights:

Anger is an energy or force which is often harmful. Anger is caused by feelings of helplessness and the need to control situations, people and consequences. Anger—when expressed in a healthy way—can foster personal growth and significance, improving relationships and changing lives.

Questions for Thought

1. Do you agree or disagree with the Foundational Insights?

2. What do these statements teach about the underlying motivations for anger?

3. How does this change or help your perspective about anger?

4. Do you ever get angry? What kinds of situations most often make you feel angry?

5. How do you really feel about your own anger? Do you see it as a friend you can trust or a foe that might destroy you? Why?

6. Why is it so hard to acknowledge your own anger?

What are you afraid might happen if you are honest or transparent about this?

What can you do to become more comfortable about this?

7. How would your life be different if you were to respond to anger in a healthy way?

What would need to change?

3
THE POWER
OF ANGER

Anger is a great force. If you control it — it can be transmuted into a
power which can move the whole world.
William Shenstone

Anger can actually be helpful. Anger is like a warning signal alerting you that something is wrong. It can provide the energy to resist emotional or physical threats. Anger can help you mobilize your resources and set appropriate limits and boundaries. Your anger can give you strength to resist threatening demands or a violation of your values.

Anger helps you overcome the fear of asserting your needs and facing conflict. Anger can be used for beneficial purposes.

And yes, anger can be harmful. As someone has wisely stated, "A man is never in worse company than when he flies into a rage and is beside himself." As Will Rogers quipped, "People who fly into a rage always make a bad landing."

William Blake wrote: "I was angry with my friend. I told my wrath, my wrath did end. I was angry with my foe; I told it not, my wrath did grow."

Unexpressed anger is not only harmful to you physically, but it plays havoc on your emotions and your spirituality. When you don't talk about your anger and the issue that upsets you, you are pretending that everything is fine and are hiding your true feelings. You end up living a lie. The Good Book says, "having put away falsehood, let each one of you speak the truth with his neighbor, for we are members one of another."[1]

Harmful anger costs you too much physically. It yields the largest increases in heart rate and blood pressure of all emotional reactions. Anger results in ulcers, cardiovascular diseases, colitis, and a depleted immune system. Not only is it damaging to the body, but anger damages mental health and relationships.

Signs indicating when anger is a problem:

- When it is too frequent.
- When it is too intense.
- When it lasts too long.
- When it leads to aggression.
- When it disturbs work or relationships.

Questions for Application

1. What is your perception of anger? Is it always wrong?
2. How did you experience anger in your family of origin? Was it expressed in a healthy or unhealthy way?
3. In what kinds of situations do you experience anger now?
4. How often do you feel angry?
5. How intense has your anger been?
6. How long does your anger last?
7. When has your anger led to aggressive behavior?
8. When has anger disturbed your work or relationships?
9. What circumstances predispose you to frustration and anger?

When Anger Wakes Up

To help you understand why it is hard to shake anger after it wakes up, you need to learn the physiological mechanism involved in anger arousal:

The amygdala—a component of the limbic system or emotional brain—mediates anger responses judging input either as rewarding or aversive (e.g., pain, threat). If an event is judged as potentially threatening, a message is sent to lower brain areas that activate the fight/flight response. This activation basically heightens sympathetic arousal in the body leading to increased breathing, heart rate, pupil dilation, and muscle tone. Blood vessels near the skin will constrict to prevent excessive bleeding in case of injury. Blood will drain from the face resulting in a pale complexion. All of these responses are mediated by nerve or electrical conduction. The reaction begins in less than a second and takes only about 3 seconds to become fully activated. Then, a hormonal surge kicks in that lasts thirty minutes. Your long-term anger response can be abbreviated when the early stage of anger arousal is interrupted.

Who's responsible for your anger? A five-year-old was showing a kindergarten classmate the new weight scale in the bathroom. "What's it for?" the visitor asked. "I don't know," the youngster replied. "All I know is, when you stand on it, it makes you very mad." You make the decision to get angry. No one can control you and your feelings. People may try to "get your goat," but you make the decision to get angry, laugh, or forget about it.

Anger Triggers

Factors that predispose anger arousal include the following:

Aversive bodily states actually increase anger arousal. Fatigue, sleep deprivation, pain, hangovers all lower the threshold of reactivity to an event that can precipitate anger. Premenstrual syndrome and low blood sugar can actually contribute to aggression.

"A sweet tooth does not translate into a sweet demeanor." Actually it accomplishes the opposite. High intakes of sugar trigger a surge of insulin that not only converts sugar just consumed but also other available sugar. This leads to depressed blood sugar levels, resulting in moodiness and triggering irritability and aggression.

Cognitive triggers: The way you perceive an event determines the extent to which you judge it as threatening provocation. Extremely rigid or biased appraisals of events prime you for over-reaction to what might normally be only a slightly irritating incident.

How you create anger:

Anger cycle #1 begins with an event or some stress that leads to Trigger Thoughts:

Events/Stress ▶

       Trigger Thoughts ▶ Anger ▼

               More Trigger Thoughts ▼

                   More Anger ▼

              More Trigger Thoughts ▼

Increases Anger and So On.

These cycles are self-perpetuating. Your self-talk can keep your anger simmering.

Anger cycle #2: Another way to arouse anger is by Trigger Thoughts that actually create some arousal or stress. This results in feelings of anger, which leads to more Trigger Thoughts, creating a stress reaction that fuels more anger.

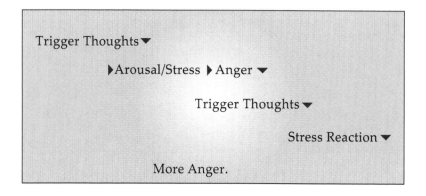

Trigger Thoughts ▼

▶Arousal/Stress ▶ Anger ▼

Trigger Thoughts ▼

Stress Reaction ▼

More Anger.

Here's an example for anger cycle #1:

A friend stands you up for a luncheon date, and you begin to think about how this friend has let you down in the past. This triggers hurt and anger and more thoughts about how this friend's behavior has disappointed you, which results in more anger.

Here's an example for anger cycle #2:

Arthur wonders if his wife will work late at the office again tonight. He imagines himself sitting alone through the news and sit-coms waiting to hear her key in the door. These thoughts trigger a sense of loneliness. He thinks the pain is her fault and converts his stressful feelings to anger. This stirs up more Trigger Thoughts as he tells himself, "She doesn't really care."

Other sources that may trigger your anger include biases. For example, you may favor certain types of inputs or interpretations of events over others. A bias leads you to interpret an event as aversive or negative. Thus you may perceive an accidental bump in the school hallway as premeditated. This kind of appraisal system makes too much of provoking events, triggering anger.

Another common bias is: "If you provoke me, it is OK for me to strike back." This type of thinking sets the stage for retaliation. A final type of misappraisal system can be called the "knuckle bias." As one adolescent put it, "The only thing they'll understand is a fist in the face." This kind of bias leads you to believe that aggressive force is the only option that has any meaningful effect. Many people today believe that violence is an acceptable way to settle disputes.

Irrational Beliefs

While biases affect how input is weighed, generalized beliefs that you may hold will see provoking input even when there is no intentional provocation. You may think that people must or should act in a certain way and when they fail to meet these standards, you get angry. (McKay et al., 1988)

Common anger-inducing beliefs include:

- Because I want it, I should get it (entitlement). "They should appreciate my work." "I should get . . ."
- It has to be fair. "Since I worked as hard as she did, I should . . ."
- I have to be right (self-righteousness). "No, it's not that way, it's . . ." "I just don't think that's right."
- "If you cared about me, you . . ." (conditional assumption). "If I was important to you, you'd . . ." "If you were my friend, you'd . . ."
- I have to be in control. (This frequently underlies jealousy.) "Are you going out dressed that way?" "I'm not leaving until you . . ."
(Gintner, p. 9.)

The important aspect about irrational beliefs is that you really believe there is a good reason for getting upset. You feel threatened and fear that something awful may happen, even when the event is minor. Or you may be dealing with low self-esteem, which can cause an overreaction to events (see Gintner, p. 10).

Impulsivity is frequently attributed to an underdeveloped defensive system. This is seen in adolescence more often than in mature adults. Defenses like sublimation (which refocuses energy into positive behavior) or rationalization (which constructs a logical justification for someone's actions) are unavailable for delaying an anger response. The impulsive person rarely quells a horrible urge by a rationalization such as "He's probably having a bad day." Rather, immature defenses such as fantasy, denial, or acting out are the major emotional regulators. Anger explosions operate like a release valve so that "you act it out" instead of "thinking it out."

Skill deficits in cognitive and behavioral areas contribute to an impulsive acting out of anger. There are ways to avoid or escape this. One way is using self-talk to guide behavior and delay responses (for example, "Wait a minute—hitting won't help right now. Take a breather").

Those with poor self-control are characterized by hot self-talk: "He thinks he can bully me . . ." Or the person ruminates about events, allowing the anger to build internally. Those with healthy self-talk think, "I'm not going to think about that now. I'm going to . . ." or entertain alternative solutions to provocation such as problem-solving.

Substance use: This addictive/obsessive behavior has a disinhibiting effect on anger and on aggression. Thus the person speaks or acts in ways that normally he or she would not even consider.

Family: An aggressive individual typically comes out of a home environment characterized by high overt conflict and low levels of positive interchanges.

Stress-current life situations: Living under conditions of chronic stress, or frequent daily hassles, takes a toll on an individual's coping resources.

A major stressful life event (such as divorce or death) on top of chronic stress (such as harsh economic conditions and unemployment) can lead to an aggressive overreaction. Example: marital discord resulting in child abuse.

Consider media reports of those who go on a murder spree after a job loss or marital separation. Who or what is responsible? The person who is angry and acts out his or her anger is responsible.

What Happens in the Process of Anger?

When someone hurts us physically or emotionally we become angry. We may flare up immediately or think about it awhile and then become angry. Something happens when we are frustrated: someone or something prevents us from reaching a goal. The anger covers up our feelings of disappointment or failure. In the short run it may keep us going. In the long run it will deplete our emotional energy. Poor self-concept, negative self-evaluations and fear lie behind the anger.

Dr. Paul Hauck outlines six levels of thought people move through in getting angry:

1. "I want something."

2. "I didn't get what I wanted and am frustrated."

3. "It is awful and terrible not to get what I want."

4. "You shouldn't frustrate me! I must have my way."

5. "You're bad for frustrating me."

6. "Bad people ought to be punished."

Apply these steps to a recent episode in which you became angry. Our perception of truth begins to break down in level 3. We don't like to be frustrated, but being frustrated is not as terrible as we think. Levels 4-6 show a retreat to irrationality and can result in uncontrolled anger as we think these unhealthy thoughts.

Why must we have our way? Who says people are bad just because they frustrate us? Who says bad people ought to be punished? Consider what God said, "Vengeance is mine."[2]

What is involved at the level of thought when anger goes bad? Cognitive distortions; irrational beliefs; false beliefs about God, what is good for us, and how we can or cannot secure significance.

Foundational Insights:

Anger is a response to fear, helplessness, frustrated goals, tense or difficult situations, false beliefs, conflicts, or stress. Triggers can increase an angry response. But when the situation or event is analyzed, one should determine whether there is a legitimate reason for getting angry. Maybe it is: "I don't like the decision that was made because _____ ." Or "I felt disrespected or misjudged by the way I was treated." The key is to identify the issue and decide whether it is valid. Then approach the situation or person to work through the matter in a healthy way.

Questions for Thought

1. When have you been angry and discovered later there was no legitimate reason for your response?

2. What triggered the anger?

3. What were your feelings/thoughts beneath the anger?

4. When did you get angry over a legitimate issue? What was the issue? Were you able to work through it effectively without harming the other person or yourself?

5. Take the following Irrational Belief Inventory.

Check which belief(s) applies to you:

I regularly think:

☐ Because I want it, I should get it (entitlement). "They should appreciate my work." "I should get . . ."

☐ It has to be fair. "Since I worked as hard as she did, I should . . ."

☐ I have to be right (self-righteousness). "No, it's not that way, it's . . ." "I just don't think that's right."

☐ "If you cared about me, you . . ." (conditional assumption). "If I was important to you, you'd . . ." "If you were my friend, you'd . . ."

☐ I have to be in control. (This frequently underlies jealousy.) "Are you going out dressed that way?" "I'm not leaving until you . . ."

(Gintner, p. 9.)

Which belief(s) do you struggle with? How much do these beliefs inhibit anger control?

Assess Your Anger Now

1. Go back and take the Anger Survey to assess your anger if you haven't already completed it.

2. Then go to the Cognitive Distortions section later in this book

and evaluate your thinking behind the anger you are struggling with.

3. Keep an anger log throughout the week. Use the log at the end of the Anger Survey. Complete the Anger Management Progress Report weekly.

4. Write out how you are developing self-awareness as you learn about anger:

   a. My top three anger triggers are:

   b. My top three areas to develop in managing anger are:

   c. The top three thinking errors that contribute to my anger escalation are:

   d. My top three coping skills for managing anger are:

4
WHEN ANGER IS GOOD

There is good anger. It is anger governed by self-control, motivated by compassion, desiring what is right versus what is wrong.
Lynette Hoy

Do you struggle with the question, "How can anything good come from anger?" You are not alone. While there are plenty of examples of harmful anger, we rarely encounter good examples.

How many times this week did you get angry? What resulted?

- yelling.

- rude or obscene remarks.

- aggression, violence.

- depression, hidden anger.

What were the consequences?

- sense of guilt, regret, or shame.

- defensiveness or thinking, "They deserved it."

- more anger, resentment.

- broken relationships.

- trouble with the law or your employer.

The premise of this book is that feelings of anger are normal and at times justified. The degree to which you become angry, the reasons for your anger, and the outcome of your anger determine whether your anger is, in fact, good.

When anger is expressed in healthy ways, it is a change agent. Anger can actually change a passive victim into someone who is confident and assertive. An aggressive person can learn self-control. Anger can motivate people to solve problems and resolve conflict. Your anger can be converted into forgiveness versus internalized as resentment.

But when anger is hidden and suppressed, it most likely will result in depression. The tendency for many religious people and leaders is to avoid the expression of anger because they believe anger is wrong in any situation. Thus anger is viewed negatively and is often denied.

In the following situation Bob writes about his struggles with anger and control:

"My anger always stayed in check at work. One day I was tested beyond imagination by a co-worker who was trying to pick a fight over who was right regarding some technical issue. This was many years ago, but it has never left me. I allowed someone of inferior intellect to gain control over me by losing my temper and yelling (in the middle of the laboratory . . . a very academic and disciplined environment). The ironic point is that my faulty thinking said anger= control, and by getting angry I gave up that one thing in my mind that was worth fighting for: control. The biggest cost is the alienation that follows. It isolates me from the very people to whom I want to be close. Instead of control, I gained loneliness."

Bob didn't get what he wanted. He also lost the respect and trust of his co-workers.

There is some truth in Phyllis Diller's quip, "Never go to bed mad. Stay up and fight." Of course, fighting is destructive and not recommended. The point Diller is making here is how important it is to bring resolution to anger and relationship conflict.

So, what is good about anger? Anger:

- gives you information about yourself, events, and people.
- helps energize you for action and faith.
- moves you to express your feelings and resolve conflict.
- enables you to assert yourself and move toward problem-solving.

What are some sensible, healthy admonitions for being "good and angry"?

1. Be angry, but put limitations on its expression in order to prevent harming yourself or others.

2. Take responsibility for your anger. Don't blame it on someone else.

3. Slow your anger down. Think through anger versus immediately acting it out.[1]

4. Don't let your anger intensify, as it will generally bring about harm.

5. Don't associate with angry people.[2]

6. Seek healthy resolution to issues.

7. Always consider the outcome of anger and how it will impact others as well as yourself.

8. Learn healthy ways to express your anger.

What happens when you encounter someone who is angry?

How You Can Handle Someone Else's Anger

We tend to get angry at someone who is angry. Why is that? We react defensively to angry people because we think their anger is wrong and threatening. What can we do to drain the anger from someone else versus provoking their anger even more?

King Solomon wrote, "a gentle answer turns away wrath, but a harsh word stirs up anger."[3]

A simple method of paraphrasing what an angry person says to you can help defuse his/her anger.

Here's an example:

Angry person: "I can't stand the stress of you interrupting me when I am working on a project. You are so inconsiderate!"

You say, "You find it very stressful when I interrupt you during an important project."

Angry person: "Yes! And furthermore, I need more peace and quiet around here."

You say, "You would like more peace and want me to stop interrupting you."

Angry person: "Yes. You seem to have gotten the message."

You say, "I appreciate you sharing this with me. In the future,

I will try to avoid interrupting you when I see you concentrating on a project."

At a later time when the person's anger has subsided, bring up the other issues that need resolution by saying, "When would be a good time for me to discuss my questions and concerns with you in the future?" and/or "I would like you to clarify what you meant by your need for more peace and quiet."

This example of paraphrasing should generally be used for the purpose of defusing and draining someone else's anger. It is not sufficient for use in cases where you need to work through a conflict with someone or deal with an unfair accusation or an abusive situation.

The premise of this book is to teach you that anger is good when turned into:

- Faith: Trusting in your Higher Power.

- Assertiveness: Speaking the truth in love.

- Problem-solving: Seeking the best solution.

- Conflict resolution: Negotiating to win-win.

- Forgiveness: Letting go of resentment.

What's in it for you?

What will you get out of controlling your anger? First of all, you will gain self-control and a sense of "personal power" (not power over others). No one will be able to make you angry or pull your strings. You will have the power to choose to be angry or not! Having "personal power" is pulling your own strings and gaining control over yourself. If you can keep cool, you are more likely to respond in ways that serve your best interests.

Look at the pros and cons of reacting to provocation with aggression. What are the positives and negatives?

If someone calls you a name and you hit him/her, you believe "they'll think twice about messing with me."

On the other hand, you may get sued or arrested for assault and battery. When you avoid responding aggressively, you gain self-respect and, most likely, respect from others. You also avoid negative consequences with the law.

Foundational Insights:

When we step back and assess the situations that cause us to feel angry, we can plan for a healthy response. When we consider the consequences for our response and the best interests of others and ourselves, we are motivated to express anger effectively and appropriately.

Questions for Thought

1. Do you really believe that not all anger is wrong, that in fact anger is sometimes good? Why or why not?

What motivates you to change how you handle anger?

2. What impact will it have when you become aware of your intentions, goals, and outcomes regarding your anger?

3. When have you considered how your anger will affect someone else?

4. What does it mean to have "personal power"? What are the pros and cons of keeping your cool and pulling your own strings? How does having "personal power" differ from control?

5. What have you learned from King Solomon's advice about responding to those who are angry? Do you agree or disagree?

5
DEFUSING ANGER BY MANAGING STRESS

There are very few certainties that touch us all
in this mortal experience, but one of the absolutes is that we will
experience hardship and stress at some point.
Dr. James Dobson

What role does stress play in anger escalation? Research has demonstrated that high stress levels precipitate angry outbursts and aggression. Take the stress inventory at the end of this chapter to learn how stress is impacting your life and emotions.

Overview of Stress: The Wikipedia Encyclopedia states that "Stress (roughly the opposite of relaxation) is a medical term for a wide range of strong external stimuli, both physiological and psychological, which can cause a physiological response called the general adaptation syndrome, first described in 1936 by Hans Selye in the Journal of Nature."

Stress and its effects

Selye was able to separate the physical effects of stress from other physical symptoms suffered by patients through his research. He observed that patients suffered physical effects not caused directly by their disease or by their medical condition.

Selye described the general adaptation syndrome as having three stages:

- alarm reaction, where the body detects the external stimulus.

- adaptation, where the body engages defensive countermeasures against the stressor.

- exhaustion, where the body begins to run out of defenses.

There are two types of stress: eustress ("positive stress") and distress ("negative stress"), roughly meaning challenge and overload. Both types may be the result of negative or positive events. If a person both wins the lottery and has a beloved relative die on the same day, one event does not cancel the other—both are stressful events. Eustress is essential to life, like exercise to a muscle; however, distress can cause disease. (Note that what causes distress for one person may cause eustress for another, depending upon each individual's life perception.) When the word stress is used alone, typically it is referring to distress. Serenity is defined as a state in which an individual is disposition-free or largely free from the negative effects of stress, and in some cultures it is considered a state that can be cultivated by various practices, such as meditation and other forms of training.

Stress can directly and indirectly contribute to general or specific disorders of body and mind. Stress can have a major impact on the physical functioning of the human body. Such stress raises the level of adrenaline and corticosterone in the body, which in turn increases the heart rate, respiration, and blood pressure and puts more physical stress on bodily organs. Long-term stress can be a contributing factor in heart failure, high blood pressure, stroke and other illnesses.

Stress is a threat to the safety and well-being of the body. In time past, the physical stress response was a means of survival: it prepared us for fight or flight. What is this so-called fight or flight reaction? It is instinctive and consists of messages sent all over the body to and from the brain. These messages alert the body of a perceived threat. In a threatening situation, we are given two options: either we can stand our ground and fight the threat or we can run away from it. The choice is made based on our perception of the situation: if we feel we have a chance of overcoming the danger (e.g., winning the fight) or not.

The various triggers for anger covered earlier are also triggers for a stress response. A stress reaction can precipitate or coincide with an angry response. Thus, avoiding triggers such as drinking, substance abuse, hot self-talk, irrational beliefs, distorted thoughts, overspending, unhealthy behavior, and any preventable stressful situations can thwart angry responses. Obviously, there are stressful circumstances in life that cannot be avoided.

Changing what you say to yourself and how you view life can greatly impact how you manage stress and anger. Your self-talk originates from your view of life and yourself. If you view life as "grab for all the gusto you can get!" based on the premise that "eat, drink, and be merry, for tomorrow we die," then you will experience more stress and anger! Why? Because you will hurry through life looking for satisfaction in anything without thinking about the consequences or caring about what is best for your life and those you love. And you will experience dissatisfaction—the opposite of what you really want! If you view life as meaningless, you will tell yourself, "what's the point?" or "why bother?" when you face responsibilities and decisions. Or if you view life as overwhelming or yourself as never measuring up, you will tell yourself, "I can't handle that" or "This is too much for me" or "I'll just fail anyway." Your negative self-talk will generate more feelings of stress, hopelessness, and less motivation for change. We call this inner talk "stress-talk." Stress-talk will cause more anger and frustration in your life. The chapters on cognitive distortions can help you challenge and change any stress-talk.

Other internal stress-talk messages occur when you try to control people. You may say to yourself, "He/she should do it my way" or "Why is she going out dressed that way?" because of your need to control. Underlying your need to control may be feelings of insecurity, jealousy, low self-worth, or the urge to teach others how to live their lives. Whatever the cause, your need for control will increase feelings of stress and anger.

How can you deal with the need to control? First, consider these negative consequences:

- You will run out of energy and feel more frustration when you try to control everything and everyone in your life.

- You will push your family and friends away from you. No one likes a controller.

- Generally, you won't get what you want when you try to control.

- In the long-run, your inner needs of security and significance won't be met.

Complete the "Am I a Controller?" inventory at the end of this chapter to see if you have this tendency.

Another form of stress-talk is blaming. You may be blaming others for your anger and disappointments in life, thinking, "if they would meet my needs I would be happy." The fact is that no one will completely meet your needs and that you have the power to make choices that will help fulfill your needs. You can take ownership of your feelings and better communicate your needs by saying to others:

"I feel angry (frustrated, disappointed, overwhelmed, hurt, or let down, etc.) when you don't listen to me (or interrupt me)."

This formula for communication helps you express your reaction and emotions without blaming. It brings up the issue and helps the other person feel less defensive.

Think about some situations when you could have used the above formula:

Situation:

I felt angry when I thought:

Identify the issue: Was it valid? Could you have made a request?

Balance your relationships and life in order to manage stress. We were made to connect with people. Relationships are very important whether you are an extrovert (outgoing) type of person or an introvert (needing more time to yourself). Having healthy, caring, significant relationships with others gives us meaning for living, encouragement, and companionship throughout our lives.

Relationships can be draining or restoring. If you are in relationships that are unhealthy because you are giving more than getting or there is too much conflict and friction, then you will feel stressed out. It could be that you tend to be codependent and need boundaries or more assertiveness in your relationships.

What about focusing on your needs and preventing negative consequences? Many times we sabotage the efforts to meet our basic needs and manage anger by engaging in activities that are unhealthy and exacerbate both stress and anger. You may think that you are decreasing stress by drinking, smoking, or using other substances when actually these habits are making your life more miserable. In the beginning of the book we discuss the fact that substance abuse increases irritability and thus is a trigger for anger. You need to decide what to change and how to make healthy choices that will improve your health, mind, emotions, spirit, and relationships. You may find comfort in the use of substances, but it will only be temporary. The long-term negative consequences will outweigh the short-term "highs" and only exacerbate feelings of anger.

How can you increase the eustress (positive stress) in your life? Take a look at your life to see how you can get revitalized. Do you have some activities that encourage and inspire you such as exercise, singing, playing an instrument, going to church, involvement in a support group, or something else meaningful or creative?

Beginning a new goal such as a class or a hobby or sport will revitalize you. What past activities would you like to reestablish? Riding your bike? Going fishing? Taking an art class? Going hiking or canoeing? These kinds of activities will create "positive stress" and refresh you! You will notice the world around you and begin to love life again!

Examine your personal pace of life with the following Stress Buster Project. See what you might need to change. Simplify your life by starting to do and be that for which you were designed. You will begin to feel more hopeful, more peaceful and encouraged as you renew your whole person, soul, and spirit.

Stress Buster Project: Building Balance into Your Life by Adjusting Your Personal Pace

Here are some questions to help you begin to prioritize your life and relieve the stress of your pace of life:

1. What is it that I need to change to make my life healthier? Stop the use of drugs, alcohol, smoking, etc.?

What needs to happen for me to stop doing things that impair my life and result in more anger and stress?

2. Is it possible to do all the things I am trying to do in the time I have?

Write down a list of the responsibilities you are performing each week:

Identify those activities that someone could help you with: Identify the activities which you might not need to do:

3. Why am I trying to do the things I have set out to do?
Of the activities listed above that you might not need to do, ask, what is the purpose of each?

4. Which of the activities you are engaged in doing do you consider worthwhile? Enjoyable? Profitable? Meaningful?

5. What do I really want to do but never seem to get around to doing?

Something creative, fun, enjoyable:

6. What changes can I make this week?

7. What can I stop doing that is not really necessary for achieving healthy goals for my life or is not really something I need to do that accomplishes the goals for myself and my family?

8. How can I embark on the goals, that I really feel are necessary for improvement of my life and family, which I never get around to doing?

What goals/activities can I begin to do in which I can use my talents and gifts?

Which healthy goals/activities have made me feel refreshed and fulfilled in the past?

9. Make a plan to reduce the stress in your life this week: Prioritize your responsibilities.

Ask someone to help you with a certain responsibility:

Stop doing something that is causing ill-effects in your life:

Stop doing something that you really don't need/want to do:

Begin to do one or two activities daily that will help enrich you physically, emotionally, and spiritually:

Maybe you are interested in how faith might decrease your stress and anger. Many people have found that God gives them an eternal perspective on life and inner strength to manage anger effectively. If you are interested in reading more about how faith affects anger, order the first edition of What's Good About Anger? or the six-part DVD series at: www.whatsgoodaboutanger.com

Progressive Relaxation

It has been proven that relaxation techniques are beneficial for reducing stress in your life and thus decreasing the resulting feelings of anger and frustration. With so many things to do, it's easy to put off taking time to relax each day. But in doing so, you miss out on the health benefits of relaxation. Relaxation can improve how your body responds to stress by:

- Slowing your heart rate, meaning less work for your heart.
- Reducing blood pressure.
- Slowing your breathing rate.
- Reducing the need for oxygen.
- Increasing blood flow to the major muscles.
- Lessening muscle tension.

After practicing relaxation skills, you may experience these benefits:

- Fewer symptoms of illness, such as headaches, nausea, diarrhea, and pain.
- Few emotional responses such as anger, crying, anxiety, apprehension, and frustration.
- More energy.
- Improved concentration.
- Greater ability to handle problems.
- More efficiency in daily activities.

Relaxed breathing

Have you ever noticed how you breathe when you're stressed? Stress typically causes rapid, shallow breathing. This kind of breathing sustains other aspects of the stress response, such as rapid heart rate and perspiration. If you can get control of your breathing, the spiraling effects of acute stress will automatically become less intense. Relaxed breathing, also called diaphragmatic breathing, can help you.

Practice this basic technique twice a day, every day, whenever you feel tense. Follow these steps:

1. **Inhale.** With your mouth closed and your shoulders relaxed, inhale as slowly and deeply as you can to the count of six. As you do that, push your stomach out. Allow the air to fill your diaphragm.

2. **Hold.** Keep the air in your lungs as you slowly count to four.

3. **Exhale.** Release the air through your mouth as you slowly count to six.

4. **Repeat.** Complete the inhale-hold-exhale cycle three to five times.

Recommended Relaxation Technique:

Experts say it's best to practice relaxation for at least twenty minutes per day. At first, practicing the following relaxation technique may seem awkward. In time, and with practice, you'll feel more comfortable with the practice and the results. Learning to relax can help prevent the escalation of anger.

Find a quiet place where you won't be disturbed. Make sure you're sitting comfortably with your back straight or lying comfortably with your arms along your sides. Close your eyes and begin focusing on your body. Slowly breathe in through your nose and out through your mouth. When thoughts and images arise in your mind, acknowledge them, and then let them go away as you bring your focus back to your breathing. Fully experience each exhale. Practice this for about five minutes or so.

Shift your focus to your body. Start with your feet. Tighten the muscles in your feet and toes, hold them tense for a couple seconds, then release the tension and let your feet relax. Next, focus on your calves. Tighten the muscles in your calves, hold them tense for a couple seconds, then release the tension and let your calves relax. Repeat this through all of your major muscle groups as you move your attention up your body. Tense your thighs, hold, and then relax. Move to your chest, hands, arms, shoulders, and finally your face.

After you have relaxed all of your muscle groups, mentally check over your body from head to toe and feel for any muscles that are still tense. If you notice a part of you that is not totally relaxed, tense it up a little, hold, and then relax. Sit, or lay, in silence with your eyes closed for twenty minutes or for as long as is comfortable.

Many people incorporate prayer during their time of relaxation.

Foundational Insights:

Making personal choices to live a healthy life-style can decrease the stress that precipitates anger. Learning relaxation techniques can slow down your physiological "fight-flight" response to anger.

Questions for Thought

1. Which of the suggestions in this chapter did you find most helpful in regard to managing anger? Why? How can you implement this principle into your life? (Be practical, not theoretical.)

2. Do you agree that the reason we can't manage our anger is because we don't want to give up control? Is this true in your life? With what results? What can you do to get this in better balance?

3. Check which kind of "stress-talk" you struggle with:

☐ "Eat, drink and be merry, for tomorrow we die."

☐ "I can't handle that."

☐ "I'll just fail anyway."

☐ "He/she should do it my way."

☐ "If he/she would meet my needs, I would be happy."

☐ Other: _____

4. How do you communicate your needs to others? Do you tend to blame or take ownership for your needs?

What steps can you take to meet your own needs and responsibilities?

5. What happened when you tried the relaxation technique? How did you feel during and afterward?

6. What other types of activities help promote relaxation for you? Listening to music? Reading?

Make time every day to relax as suggested. Plan for times of relaxing activities during the week as well.

7. Ask yourself about your need to control. What about trying for the next two weeks to let those you have been trying to control make their own choices? Wouldn't it be refreshing to see them making the right choices according to their own volition? Wouldn't it be a relief to no longer have to nag, remind, manipulate, or force someone to do what you think is best? Wouldn't it be a relief to just concentrate on your responsibilities and goals, and mutually work with your spouse on family goals?

Do You Fit the Description of a Controller or Abuser? Answer these questions honestly: Do you ever:

☐ Embarrass, make sarcastic remarks or fun of your spouse/partner in front of your friends or family?

☐ Put down your spouse's accomplishments or goals?

☐ Demonstrate extreme jealousy?

☐ Make your spouse feel unable to make decisions?

☐ Yell at him/her, let your temper get out of control?

☐ Use intimidation or threats to gain compliance from him/her?

☐ Tell him/her that he/she is nothing without you?

☐ Treat him/her roughly—grab, push, pinch, shove, or hit him/her?

☐ Call him/her several times a night or show up to make sure he/she is where he/she said he/she would be?

☐ Use drugs or alcohol as an excuse for saying hurtful things or abusing him/her?

☐ Blame him/her for how you feel or act?

☐ Pressure him/her sexually for things he/she isn't ready for?

☐ Show cruelty to animals?

☐ Make him/her feel like there is "no way out" of the relationship?

☐ Prevent him/her from doing things he/she wants—like spending time with his/her friends or family?

☐ Try to keep him/her from leaving after a fight or leave him/her somewhere after a fight to "teach him/her a lesson"?

Do you almost always need (with your partner):

☐ To have things done your way? To have the last word?

☐ To make your point understood?

☐ To behave negatively (yell, use obscenities, put-downs, or name calling or force) when you don't get your way?

☐ To behave negatively when you feel misunderstood?

☐ To demonstrate how right you are?

☐ To show how wrong your partner is?

☐ To have your wishes granted?

☐ To react negatively when your partner disappoints you?

☐ To respond with an outburst of anger when your partner misunderstands or disappoints you?

Do you cause your partner to:

☐ Sometimes feel scared of you because you make threatening gestures or indirect threats or throw or break objects?

☐ Make excuses for your behavior?

☐ Believe that he/she is the only one who needs to change, not you?

☐ Avoid conflict and never disagree with you in order to "keep the peace"?

☐ Feel like no matter what he/she does, he/she can't please you?

☐ Placate you by doing whatever you want and rarely doing what he/she wants?

☐ Stay with you because he/she is afraid of the consequences of leaving you?

If you have checked any of these symptoms, you have the characteristics of a controller. If you checked any of these symptoms — (physical, sexual abuse, verbal threats, outbursts or rageful behavior, harassment, manipulation by fear, cruelty to animals) — you fit the description of a batterer and abuser with severe anger and control issues. You need help.

Explore these questions and challenge yourself: What makes you need to force your partner to grant your every wish and expectation? How does it make you feel when someone forces or pressures you to do something you don't want to do? What kind of love do you want from your spouse/partner? Love is real when it is freely given. You need to explore what is driving you to control and/or batter your spouse. Call a professional counselor. Contact a local domestic violence agency for Batterer's Intervention classes (in the USA, National Domestic Violence Agency at 1-800-799-7233).

For more resources visit www.counselcareconnection.org and www.whatsgoodaboutanger.com

THE STRESS OF ADJUSTING TO CHANGE:

Circle the events occurring over the past two years and total the points.

EVENTS	SCALE OF IMPACT
Death of a spouse	100
Divorce	73
Marital separation	65
Jail term	63
Death of close family member	63
Personal injury or illness	53
Marriage	50
Fired at work	47
Marital reconciliation	45
Retirement	45
Change in health of family member	44
Pregnancy	40
Sex difficulties	39
Gain of new family member	39
Business readjustment	39
Change in financial state	38
Death of close friend	37

Change to different line of work 36

Change in number of arguments with spouse 35

Mortgage (mod-high) 31

Foreclosure of mortgage or loan 30

Change in responsibilities at work 29

Son or daughter leaving home 29

Trouble with in-laws 29

Outstanding personal achievement 28

Wife begins or stops work 26

Begin or end school 26

Change in living conditions 25

Revision of personal habits 24

Trouble with boss 23

Change in work hours or conditions 20

Change in residence 20

Change in school 20

Change in recreation 19

Change in church activities 19

Change in social activities 18

Loan 17

Change in sleeping habits 16

Change in number of family gatherings 15

Change in eating habits 15

Vacation 13

Christmas 12

Minor violations of the law 11

Determine which events have occurred in your life over the past two years, and add up your total stress score. If your total score is under 150, you are less likely to be suffering the effects of cumulative stress. If it is between 150 and 300, you may be suffering from chronic stress, depending on how you perceived and coped with the particular life events that occurred. If your score is over 300, it is likely you are experiencing some detrimental effects of cumulative stress. Please note that the degree to which any particular event is stressful to you will depend on how you perceive it.

Resource: Holmes/Rahe (1967). The Social Readjustment Rating Scale.

6
HANDLING ANGER
EFFECTIVELY

Anyone can become angry. That is easy. But to be angry with the right person, to the right degree, at the right time, for the right purpose and in the right way—that is not easy.

Aristotle

When you are overcome with anger, you may think it's impossible to have self-control. Let's take a look at some examples of people who experienced being "good and angry." Bob wrote the following in answer to the question, "How did you recently control your anger?"

"I stopped the cycle. When I missed seeing the trigger setup early enough to just avoid the trap, I still know what I feel like when I am starting to get angry. When I start to feel even a little like that, I just call for a time-out or I pause and remind myself of how important it is to remain in control of myself, not the other person.

"Recently I was having an emotionally charged discussion with my girlfriend. This of course means that we both felt strongly about the topic and had opposing viewpoints. I was able to look ahead and see how the conversation was going to unfold, so I stopped talking.

I started asking questions to understand her viewpoint. This is much easier to do when I remind myself that she is not trying to hurt me, she really loves me, and she wants the best for both of us. It's amazing what some corrected thinking can accomplish."

Notice how this student applies a time-out, uses clarifying questions, corrects his thinking, and considers the potential escalation. These steps and skills keep anger and conflict from escalating. This is a healthy example of how to work through anger.

Many centuries ago a righteous man named Nehemiah wrote about an incident when he became angry: "I was very angry when I heard their outcry and these words. I took counsel with myself, and I brought charges against the nobles and the officials. I said to them, 'You are exacting interest, each from his brother.' And I held a great assembly against them."[1]

Nehemiah felt "very angry" when he heard about his countrymen's dilemma (they were being exploited by the rich). He took time out to ponder the situation and how to approach it. He then went on to confront the nobles and officials. We see here that not all anger is wrong; there is a righteous anger, and it would be wrong not to act on it. As Aristotle said, "Anyone can become angry. That is easy. But to be angry with the right person, to the right degree, at the right time, for the right purpose and in the right way—that is not easy." What is the right way to handle anger? Here are some steps to consider.

Initial Awareness of Hurt or Anger

Too often we become extremely angry before we even recognize that we are angry. Early awareness is key. What are the elements of such early awareness?

1. Recognize the underlying feelings of tension, sadness, fear, frustration, hurt, rejection, etc.

2. Take a break to reflect. Be "slow to anger."[2]

3. Many find it helpful to pray about the problem, seeking spiritual help and guidance.

4. Identify the issue. Decide whether you are distorting the truth about the event or person.

What are you angry about?

What did the other person do that hurt or frustrated you? Think about the behavior that bothered you. Don't make judgments about others' motives.

5. Evaluate whether the issue is valid. Ask, "do I have the right to be angry?" Sometimes we do, but sometimes we don't.

6. Address the issue/problem, and express your feelings: "I was frustrated/hurt/angry when you forgot about our appointment."

How are we to go about doing this?

- Establish a plan of action: "I would like to request that you call me the next time you are going to be late."

- Provide options for change: "Please take a time-out when you begin to get angry." "Please treat me with respect."

- Negotiate a resolution: "What do you want to do about disciplining the children?"

- Plan a time-frame: "I would like to see changes made over the next month."

- Express how you will help the situation: "I will call a time-out if I think the conflict is getting too hot." "I will make my requests respectfully rather than nagging you in the future." Learn to handle your anger with assertiveness (see the chapter on "Anger and Assertiveness").

7. Get guidance from a pastor, counselor, or trustworthy confidante.

8. Put the issue in perspective. Ask yourself: "Is this issue really worth getting upset over and worth bringing up? Or can I let go of it in light of the fact that I may have misunderstood the person? Or maybe the issue/situation is just not that important and I can overlook it."

9. Forgive and forget. Forgiveness brings resolution and is a step toward reconciliation.

Problem-solving

Anger is a result of feeling that you are helpless in a given situation. You can't solve the problem. The problem is too big, overwhelming, or painful. Difficulties come in all sizes and shapes, and you seem to be having more than your fair share. You may ask, "Why is life so difficult and hard? And why do some people seem to have it easy?"

Establish a plan of action. Write out options and solutions that will help you resolve the problem. You would do well to consider the following:

- What can you learn about the issue you are facing?

- What can you do about this problem? List all reasonable options, and then choose one or two.

- Try out one of the options. You can always apply another option if your first choice is not working out. Evaluate how it is affecting you and others.

- How can someone help you? Ask for counsel.

- What resources are available to resolve your problem?

- What support can you ask for or make use of?

Thinking Ahead Reminders

Here are some ideas and questions to tell yourself before and during a conflict to maintain self-control:

"Keep your breathing even."

"What is it that I have to do?"

"Take it one step at a time."

"Stick to the issue and don't take it seriously."

"What's going to happen if . . ."

"Do I need to be cool so I'm not the fool?"

"Is it really worth it?"

"Will this make a difference in a week?"

"What are some things I could say or do?"

(Gintner, p. 22-23).

Write these down on a 3x5 card, then review and keep them in your wallet or purse.

Foundational Insights:

Anger can be expressed appropriately, assertively and respectfully resulting in a healthy expression of feelings, dialogue with others and problem-solving.

Questions for Thought

1. Look back at a recent problem when you became angry. Was the problem really a legitimate one? Was it worth discussing and trying to resolve?

2. Of the "Thinking ahead reminders," which would help you cool down before or during a provoking situation?

3. What specific steps would you be willing to take (or have you taken) in the Handling Anger Effectively model to work through your anger?

4. Do the problem-solving steps make sense? When you face an issue, do you think, "What choices/options do I/we have?" or do you think, "It's my way or the highway?" What needs to happen for you to become an "option-thinker"?

5. Which steps in the Handling Anger Effectively are most difficult for you?

6. At this point in the book, how would you rate your motivation to change and manage anger? (Circle one)

Very motivated. Moderately motivated.
Somewhat motivated. Not really motivated.

How does knowing there are various healthy ways to express your anger (time-out, communication and problem-solving options) help motivate you to change?

7
ANGER AND ASSERTIVENESS

Do not be angry with me if I tell you the truth.
Socrates

Assertiveness is not aggressive or passive. Assertive people express their thoughts and feelings forthrightly without getting squashed or squashing others in the process.

Some who read this book might get the impression that one should never get angry—the risk is just too great. That, of course, is not the case. There are legitimate reasons for getting angry! Sometimes we rationalize and defend why we had an outburst. Other times we may try our hardest to not ever be angry.

Having your anger under control does not mean you have to be a wallflower—or, worse, a doormat—that you never disagree with anyone, never stand up for yourself, never confront someone and tell him or her that he or she is wrong. Handling anger the right way, with self-control, does not mean that you should stuff all angry feelings and never express them or be assertive.

Many people act out their anger aggressively, thinking they are just being assertive. The truth is that assertive behavior and communication are not aggressive, as we will explain later on. You may struggle with "acting out" your anger in harmful ways and thus, are experiencing legal, work, or relationship consequences. Making the choice to control the aggression and/or verbal outbursts will take determination and application of new behaviors and better ways to communicate.

Some of you may be indirect about expressing your feelings and needs. It's important to know that good anger is often assertive—communicating reasonable requests and opinions.

Maybe you find this difficult. Perhaps as a child you were taught that it is self-centered to talk about yourself or to express your feelings. Or you may have grown up in a volatile environment where angry outbursts were the norm. Thus, you learned to react with "fits of rage" or out of fear—to hide your anger.

You may not be direct about your opinions or disagreements because you fear people will be put off or that it will just cause a conflict. You may end up being so indirect that nearly all the time you let others speak for you. This type of communication tends to result in frustration and hidden anger.

As an indirect or passive person you may share your thoughts and feelings in a roundabout way and are apt to sound something like this: "They just laid off most of my department . . . It's kind of . .

. . Well, you know. . . . But what can you do?" When you can't express your wants openly, you have to hint—"It looks like a nice day . . . our neighbors went to play tennis" or "The newspaper mentioned an arts and crafts show this Sunday"—and hope your friend or spouse will pick up on it.

You may be a person who doesn't give a hoot about what others think. You may give them the finger, shout, or threaten when they don't meet your expectations or cross you in some way. You may struggle with "hot self-talk" and come out swinging when someone provokes you.

If you are non-assertive or passive it's difficult to decide when to stand up for your "reasonable rights" and state your opinion and when to go the extra mile in considering others' interests. You may end up apologizing for someone else's mistakes. When someone spills their coffee on you, you say you're sorry for being in the wrong place. When someone puts you down, you pretend you didn't hear the remark.

In either case, for those who are aggressive or passive, assertiveness is a healthy skill you can use effectively to defuse and work through anger.

A WORKING DEFINITION OF ASSERTIVENESS

What is assertiveness? It's a way of confronting an unpleasant or difficult situation without getting squashed or squashing others in the process. When you use assertiveness you can negotiate reasonable changes by stating directly what you think, feel, and want. Assertiveness builds intimacy, solves interpersonal problems, and increases honesty, valid requests, and legitimate refusals in your relationships. Assertiveness gives you the opportunity to air your grievances and frustrations in a healthy way instead of burying them or eventually blowing up.

Assertiveness is right!

I (Ted Griffin) can testify to the power and benefit of godly assertiveness, in this case my wife's. When I was tearing my family apart with selfish, destructive anger, my wife was able, with the courage God provides, to come to the point where she could at appropriate times tell me, "I won't allow you to talk to me in that way," then end the conversation until I had cooled down. Or she would leave the house, with the kids, leaving me alone at home to consider how my anger was affecting our family. In these and other ways her gentle but firm assertiveness made me see what my anger was doing to myself and to everyone in our home. Though I didn't always like her standing up to me at the time, looking back I can see that God used it to get my attention and to help me see how I was wrong and how I needed to change.

When I (Lynette) was first married, I would shut down and give the "cold shoulder" whenever I felt hurt by my husband. This brought a great deal of distress to our relationship because he could not understand what was wrong with me. One time he said, "Our relationship is more important than any issue. We need to work this out no matter what." It was obvious that I needed to learn how to directly communicate issues and any anger I was harboring in a healthier manner.

Of course, there are a number of alternatives to healthy assertiveness. You can fake your feelings, suffer silently, retreat, manipulate, or demand your way in a fit of rage. Ultimately these options are self-defeating, harmful to you and others resulting in negative consequences.

PRACTICAL STRATEGIES FOR BEING APPROPRIATELY ASSERTIVE

One of the keys to making assertiveness work for you while also making it palatable for others is to combine it with active listening. Listening involves hearing and paraphrasing back what others say to you. It gives you the opportunity to pick up on their viewpoints and continue the dialogue. You don't have to agree with their opinions, but active listening will show that you value and respect them. This will increase the likelihood that others will take time to listen to you.

Begin summarizing what people say to you with phrases such as:

- "In other words . . ."
- "Let me get this straight . . ."
- "So you felt that . . ."
- "What I hear you saying is . . ."
- "If I understand you correctly . . ."
- "Would you say that . . . ?"
- "Do I understand you to mean . . . ?"

Make certain that your paraphrase is brief and includes the facts and feelings the person is expressing. Some sample paraphrases might be:

- "You were really scared when the dog ran in front of the car."
- "You feel frustrated because I missed our appointment."

When you can summarize what someone has said to you, you will clarify what they are saying and keep the dialogue from getting heated.

Still, the most difficult aspect of communication comes when you take the risk to talk about your opinions, feelings, and needs. Don't let fear or anger get in the way! Learning assertive communication skills is the next step. Here are some examples of ways of assertiveness that will help you express your opinions, confront others, state your feelings, or make requests:

1. Stating your preference or opinion: "My preference is _____."
   "What I'd like is _____ ."

2. Expressing your feelings: "I feel _____ when
   _____ ."

3. Making requests: "This movie is not what I hoped it would be. I would like to leave."

4. Disagreeing with someone: "I disagree with you when you say
   _____ ."

5. Saying yes or no without making excuses: "I am unable to come
   to lunch."

6. Using "I" statements for confronting: "I feel _____ when
   you _____ because _____ ."

Here is an assertiveness approach you can apply when you need
to bring up an issue. It's called the ASERT Model:

- Approach the person calmly and with respect.

- State the problem. Think over and state the facts of the
  problem.

- Express yourself. State your feelings.

- Request change and feedback. Specify one behavior change.
  Then listen to the other person's thoughts and opinions.

- Talk it out. Paraphrase the other person's ideas. Discuss the
  consequences, considerations, and options.

Write out recent interactions you have had with people in which
you could have been less demanding or less passive. Then, using
the ASERT model, rewrite the scenario using the paraphrasing and
assertiveness skills.

Resolve to start trying your newly acquired skills this week:

- When an acquaintance asks you for a favor that conflicts
  with your schedule, just say, "I wish I could help you, but I
  have another appointment."

- When you're standing in line and someone moves in front of
  you, say, "I believe I was first in line."

- When your friend owes you money—money you could use—say, "Would you please return the money you borrowed two weeks ago?"

- When you receive a bill that is unusually high for the service you received, ask for a refund or partial credit.

- When someone is rude to you, talk to them privately, asking them to treat you with respect in the future.

- When someone is talking about his or her opinions or beliefs, listen respectfully and then, freely share yours.

Assertiveness need not be a painful exercise of skills. You can get something out of communicating more directly with others. You can direct your anger into a healthy exchange of words leading to a resolution of problems. Aristotle wrote, "Many a friendship is lost for lack of speaking." Speaking up will help you build closer relationships with others and gain more confidence in yourself! Just think—no more hinting, raging, manipulating, forcing or demanding your way! Instead you can state your ideas, thoughts, and feelings confidently while at the same time managing your anger!

To be assertive in the ways we have been talking about is not easy. It takes wisdom (what to say and when to say it), patience, discernment, and above all courage.

Dealing with Difficult People: There are times when you will encounter people who are difficult and overbearing. Here are some suggestions (from Feindler and Ecton) for handling these situations.

1. *The broken record technique: Rehearse making your requests in a firm but calm voice when someone does not respond to you.* "I want my money back . . . just give me my money back . . . all I want is my money

back . . ." It is critical to rehearse this prior to a situation in which you expect to encounter resistance and to help you maintain composure and self-control. Remember to not raise your voice.

2. When someone is engaging in annoying behavior, "ignoring" or not reacting may be the best course of action. Ignoring may lower the probability that it will occur again. However, this technique must be applied carefully since the other party may become more obnoxious. Ignoring includes: making no eye contact with the party and maintaining a neutral facial expression; attending to something else or the positive behaviors of the others in the room; as soon as the other party stops acting obnoxiously, attend to him/her.

3. Fogging. This technique is a way of confusing a provoking individual by appearing to lightheartedly agree with him or her. For example, a fogging response to someone who criticizes your clothing might be, "You really think I have no taste." A fogging response helps you maintain control by not taking a comment seriously. It also breaks the escalation cycle by side-stepping an aggressive counterresponse.

(Gintner, pp. 40-42; Feindler and Ecton)

Foundational Insights

Anger can be communicated in acceptable and even loving ways. Anger can be expressed as a request, a boundary, an opinion, a decision, or a question. When you communicate anger with respect, you will have more success in resolving issues, meeting your needs, and building healthy relationships.

Questions for Thought

1. Did you find the working definition of assertiveness helpful or unrealistic? Why?

2. Which of the "Practical Strategies for Being Appropriately Assertive" did you find most helpful? How can you implement this in your life?

3. How can you use the ASERT Model effectively? Write out a situation(s) in which you will do this. When will you begin?

4. How will the skill of assertiveness help you develop your ability to manage your anger and your behavior?

8
MANAGING
CONFLICT

I don't have to attend every argument I'm invited to.
Author Unknown

Whenever you are angry, you are dealing with conflict as well; and every time you experience real conflict, you also, at least to some extent, on some level, feel anger. Remember, not all anger is bad, and neither is all conflict.

Conflict is an inevitable part of life, work, and relationships: miscommunication between a worker and a boss; an argument between a husband and wife over finances; aggravation when a driver cuts you off or somebody at church is mad at you and refuses to speak to you. At work, what if a co-worker doesn't meet the deadline for his or her part of a combined project? How should you respond when your boss asks you to do something clearly unethical? Do you hold your tongue, wait to see what will happen, or confront, defend, maybe even blow up?

At home, what if a teenage son or daughter refuses to stop using foul language? What if a husband can't account for missing funds nearly every week but insists he has not fallen back into a gambling addiction? What if a mother refuses to let her ex-husband see their children even though the judge said he has visitation rights? If you find yourself in one of these situations, do you hold back, or do you protest, fight, and insist on your rights?

Conflict can result in either problem-solving and resolution or all-out war! How we approach conflict greatly impacts the outcome. Having the right mind-set going into it won't guarantee peaceful resolution, but having a wrong mind-set will bring certain failure and continuing tension. As long we live on earth, we will experience conflict! And that's not always bad.

GOOD REASONS TO ACCEPT AND FACE CONFLICT

- To stand against wrong. For example, if you believe abortion is wrong, participating in a pro-life hike though protesters may be there; holding a teenage son or daughter who missed curfew accountable (or following through on the threatened consequences); going to court because you received a traffic ticket unfairly.

- To protect someone. For example, if a man is physically abusing his wife or child.

- Because the situation, realistically and practically, just can't continue the way it is. For example, your marriage won't last much longer, or your boss may soon fire you.

- Because of a clear sense of urgency or responsibility. For example, William Wilberforce's long but successful battle to end slavery in the British Empire in the nineteenth century.

- To seek and experience resolution and/or reconciliation. You're ready to make peace (to confess the ways you contributed to the conflict, forgive, negotiate), and you're pretty sure the other party is too.

- Because you know you need to make right your previous
  response or behavior during a conflict—to confess your
  faults, resolve the anger, ask forgiveness, etc.

THE IMPORTANCE OF COMPASSION WHEN FACING CONFLICT

What is compassion? It is the ability to enter into the mind and heart of another, to share his sorrow, to know him "from within," thus giving rise to mercy and understanding.

In the Revelations of Divine Love Julian of Norwich calls compassion a wound. It is so because human experience teaches us that if we love we suffer. It's therefore easier not to love, for if we do we give the other power to hurt us. The pains of those we love become our own, and the more we love the more we open ourselves to possible rejection, with its attendant emotions. If we love we "feel" for others, and the more we widen our hearts to include all, the more we shall find ourselves bearing the sorrows of the world. (Elizabeth Ruth Obbard "Magnificat" pp 47, 49-50.)

A definition: Compassion means feeling what the other person feels, feeling with him or her, being able to put yourself in his or her shoes, caring enough to see his or her side.

The Holy Bible tells us to "Put on . . . compassion, kindness, humility, meekness, and patience, bearing with one another and, if one has a complaint against another, forgiving each other. . . . And above all these put on love, which binds everything together in perfect harmony."[1]

When facing conflict we face three crucial choices, and our answers make all the difference.

- Relationship or winning? If the latter, sooner or later you will lose the relationship. This is not a game!

- Connect or conquer? The first is servanthood, the second pride.

- Love or dominate? Couples often quote the following at their weddings, "Love is patient and kind; love does not envy or boast; it is not arrogant or rude. It does not insist on its own way; it is not irritable or resentful."[2]

If a wrong, selfish attitude isn't put aside, the conflict will only increase.

Practical Strategies for Managing Conflict

Step 1: When you clash or disagree with another person, one way to prevent escalation is to take a time-out to consider the issues and your response. Don't feel pressured to resolve the situation immediately. Withdraw from the person, not huffily or in condescension, but with kind words to the effect, "It's probably best if we talk about this later, when we've both cooled down and have had a chance to think over what's bothering us and what we really want to say." But don't make the time-out open-ended; try to decide when you will get back together to talk (in ten minutes? tomorrow over dinner? Wednesday night after work?). Use the time-out to pray and determine what concerns you have or what requests you might make.

Step 2: Sum up what the other person says by paraphrasing his or her demands, viewpoints, and comments. Most people don't listen well and tend to react defensively when engaged in conflict. Summarizing what someone says doesn't mean agreement with the other person's opinion or request, but it does demonstrate that you are listening, that you care and are trying to understand.

- "In other words, you were not able to make your deadline, and you hope I can finish the project.""What I hear you saying is that you want me to charge this customer 25 percent more than the normal cost."

Step 3: Communicate your need and viewpoint graciously but firmly.

- "I was able to complete my part of the project, but I do not have time to take on your portion as well."

- "I find that overcharging customers places me in an ethical dilemma, one that I believe is wrong. I cannot carry out this task."

Application: Write out a scenario in which you experienced conflict at work. Envision how you could respond by using the time-out and sum-up skills and communicating your viewpoint.

Now do the same for a situation at home or in another setting.

Applying the sum-up skills and seeking wisdom will afford you greater opportunity for success in the workplace and in all your relationships.

Question: How can I control my anger when someone (a "downer") is unfairly blaming or judging me?

Answer: Here are some steps to take. First of all, listen attentively to what is being said. Try to understand and clarify the issue and don't defend yourself against character judgments, labeling, etc., until you've dealt with the issue and you both have cooled down.

Example:

Downer: "You didn't complete that project on time (or finish the room, house-cleaning, etc.)! You are just lazy and irresponsible!"

You: "You think I am irresponsible because I didn't finish the project. Is that right?"

Downer: "Yes! I could have finished the project myself along with everything else I am doing! You just don't care!"

You: "You think I don't care because I didn't finish the project; so you think you should have done it. I want to explain to you what happened. Are you willing to listen to me?"

Downer: "Yes. But I don't think you can give me any excuses for your irresponsibility."

You: "I didn't finish the project because the kids had some unexpected needs (or other responsibilities/clients at work took precedence). I know that you are disappointed but I now have time to work on the project."

Downer: "OK. But, I'm still pretty angry about this."

You (now work toward resolution and confrontation about the character judgments): "I will do the project and have it done in a few days. But in the future, I am requesting that you refrain from making character judgments about me when you have a problem with my work."

Downer: "What do you mean by that?"

You: "I don't like being labeled irresponsible and lazy. When you need to approach me about some issue in the future, please keep to the issue—i.e. the behavior that bothers you and your feelings about it. This will help me feel respected and improve our relationship."

Foundational Insights:

Conflict is normal and a process that both parties, when willing, can work through. When conflict management skills along with compassion and empathy are applied to disputes, relationships can improve and successful resolution is possible.

Questions for Thought

1. What conflicts are you currently facing, or should you be facing, that it would be right for you to accept and handle?

How will you go about this?

2. Which of the "Practical Strategies for Managing Conflict" do you find the hardest? Why?

3. Have you been seeking to resolve some conflict but the other person is unwilling?

Have you taken any of the steps from the model? What should be the next step, and when will you take it?

4. Take the empathy inventory. How can working on empathy skills—putting yourself in someone else's shoes—help you manage conflict more effectively?

9
TURN YOUR ANGER INTO FORGIVENESS

Resentment is like taking poison and waiting for the other person to die.
Malachy McCourt

It's challenging to think about forgiving people who have hurt us, isn't it? We often don't want to let go of the painful memories of abuse, put-downs, broken promises and harsh words. I (Lynette) can remember when one of my sisters refused to give me my portion of our father's inheritance. I felt hurt and angry. It was difficult to forgive her, but in time I did. The question is, how can we unlock the door of forgiveness? First we need to understand some facts:

- Forgiveness, though difficult, is possible.

- Forgiveness is vital to resolving anger.

- Forgiveness is the road to personal healing and reconciliation with God and others.

- Forgiveness is an ongoing process.

- Forgiveness emulates the highest quality of humanity.

- Forgiveness sets you free from the past.

The Challenge of Forgiveness

Talking about forgiveness causes us to reflect on some very personal, hurtful experiences in our lives. We don't want to think about those times, and we find ourselves struggling to resolve the memories of pain and inflicted wounds by others.

What are some of the most challenging things to forgive?

People who are manipulative, abusive, irresponsible, who lie, cheat, are arrogant, disrespectful or inconsiderate? Forgiveness is a difficult topic because it calls us as human beings to a higher standard . . . the standard of grace and mercy. But when we don't forgive . . . we run into a greater human dilemma: that of unforgiveness . . . where the pain of resentment and bitterness flows through our veins, quenching our spirits, breeding a cynicism about life, people, and God. Unforgiveness encases us in a miserable existence, changing our perception of the world and people from positive to negative, causing us to withdraw, priming us to see the world and people as hostile.

How would you define Forgiveness?

Here are some ideas:
- letting go of the blame.
- ceasing resentment.
- pardoning.

Forgiveness cancels a debt someone owes us and restores relationships and is the only solution in a world ridden with sin and evil to help us start over with people and with God. Forgiveness gives us the opportunity to express love and grace to others.

What Forgiveness is and isn't

Forgiveness is a choice, not a feeling. Forgiveness is not fair, it is not easy, and it is hard work. Forgiveness is when you decide to let someone else off the hook—when you elect to not get paid back or take revenge for a wrongdoing. When you withhold punishment. Forgiveness is not turning a blind eye or ignoring what happened.

Forgiveness is not forgetting or denying what happened. Forgiveness is not the same as reconciliation. Forgiveness doesn't justify, approve or excuse the offense or offender. Forgiveness doesn't always remove the consequences of the offense from the offender. Forgiveness is a process that may include confrontation and exhortation.

Why we need Forgiveness

The state of anger creates the need to forgive. As soon as we become angry at someone or something we need the sweet relief of forgiveness, not only to grant it to others but to receive it for ourselves. We need forgiveness to bring our lives back into a state of harmony and peace.

What do religious leaders and writers have to say about the importance and process of forgiveness? Phillip Yancey wrote: "Forgiveness is another way of admitting, 'I'm human, I make mistakes, I want to be granted that privilege and so I grant you that privilege'. Forgiveness breaks the cycle. It does not settle all questions of blame and justice and fairness: to the contrary, often it evades those questions. But it does allow relationships to start over. In that way, said Solzhenitsyn, we differ from all animals. It is not our capacity to think that makes us different, but our capacity to repent, and to forgive. Only humans can perform that most unnatural act; and by doing so only they can develop relationships that transcend the relentless law of nature."

There are some who place perimeters on forgiveness. Dennis Prager is a religious Jew who explains why Jews can not forgive the Nazis—"God himself does not forgive a person who has sinned against a human being unless that human being has been forgiven by his victim. Therefore, people can never forgive murder, since the one person who can forgive is gone, forever." Mr. Prager claims that the reason Christians forgive with such ease is because "the belief that God loves everyone, no matter how evil, makes it impossible for a believing Christian to hate evil people and therefore difficult to fight them" (Prager 226, 229). Christians are told to "forgive each other, just as in Christ God forgave you."[1]

Buddhism is another religion that teaches to forgive, but Buddhists make an important distinction: that one should forgive but never forget because forgetting would allow it to happen again. Buddhists teach to always have compassion for your fellow man and never to act violently towards another (Ricard 235).

Dr. Amir Ali writes that Islam teaches the following steps in seeking forgiveness:

(1) Recognize the offense before those against whom the offense was committed and before God.

(2) Commit one-self to not repeat the offense.

(3) Do whatever needs to be done to rectify the offense (within reason) and ask pardon of the offended party.

(4) Ask God for forgiveness.

Stories of Forgiveness

Dith Pran is a survivor from the genocide in Cambodia that occurred under the rule of the Khmer Rouge. Pran places the blame on the leaders of the Khmer Rouge and not on the men who committed the murders. He says, "Pulling away from the Khmer Rouge leadership, I can forgive the soldiers of the Khmer Rouge, those who actually did the killing, although I can never forget what they did." The reason he can forgive the soldier is because he feels that the soldiers of the Khmer Rouge were dragged out of the forest, brainwashed, taught to kill, and forced to kill. If they did not follow orders, their families would have been killed along with them. Pran says that they were very poor and uneducated, and extremely afraid of dying. Pran does not take all responsibility off of the soldiers and place it on to the leaders; rather he says that he can forgive the lowly soldier because he can understand his situation (Pran 231).

One outstanding example of forgiveness occurred years ago when Corrie ten Boom, a Dutch Christian, was speaking at a church about God's forgiveness. In the audience was a former Nazi officer who had abused her and her sister during their imprisonment in Germany. He was one of the cruelest guards. He stated he was now a Christian too and asked her for forgiveness. Corrie resisted. Face to face with one of her captors, she felt unable to act.

Then she remembered that Jesus said, "If you do not forgive men their trespasses, neither will your Father in heaven forgive your trespasses." In obedience to God, she thrust her hand toward him and said, 'I forgive you, brother!' I cried. 'With all my heart.'

Former Watergate convict Chuck Colson tells about a Mrs. Washington who—during a graduation ceremony for inmates completing a Prison Fellowship program—rushed to the stage to wrap her arms around a graduating inmate, declaring, "This young man is my adopted son." Everyone had tears in their eyes, for they knew that this young man was behind bars for the murder of Mrs. Washington's daughter.

Accounts like this are amazing! How can people like Dith Pran, Corrie ten Boom and Mrs. Washington endure such great injustices and then turn around to forgive the villains? Because each followed his/her conscience, beliefs and decision to forgive.

Forgiveness cancels a debt someone owes us and restores the relationship. It is the only solution in a world ridden with sin and evil to help us start over with people and with God.

Months after the incident with one of my sisters, I felt convicted to forgive her. I knew I had to let go of the anger. I wrote and told her how much I wanted to reconcile with her. It was not until thirteen years later that she and I finally reunited.

So how can you and I practically forgive someone who has hurt us? Here are some Steps to Forgiveness. Applying these steps to our lives can deliver us from bitterness and help us work toward forgiveness:

1. **Discover forgiveness:** When you discover and experience forgiveness deeply in your own life, you have a foundation to offer forgiveness to those who have offended you. Many find God's forgiveness helps them forgive others also.

2. **Choose to forgive:** You must make the decision to let go of bitterness and revenge and forgive others.

3. **Renew your mind:** Challenge your mind with the truth and about how you need to be forgiven too. You may consider seeking your Higher Power for help in forgiving.

4. **Grant mercy:** Empathize with those who have injured you. Mrs. Washington's acceptance of her daughter's killer was based on her faith and decision to grant forgiveness and mercy.

5. **Remember—forgiveness is a process:** If you are stuck in unforgiveness, you can talk and pray with a confidante, a pastor, or a counselor to help you deal with the resentment and hurt you still feel. This will provide a context for release (of the painful feelings you are experiencing), support, and a better understanding of the person and situation.

When others hurt or abuse us, when they disrespect or humiliate us, we can forgive them as Mrs. Washington did.

So don't think that your anger should be stuffed down, negated, or turned into bitterness. Your anger is an emotion and force that can be useful. You can decide to forgive because that is a mechanism for resolving the hurts and the unfairness of life. It is the only way to free yourself from the past and from the inner turmoil that bitterness causes.

Guidelines for Reconciliation and Forgiving

1. Deal constructively with the root cause of anger toward the offending party.

    a. Ask: What am I angry about? What is my responsibility? What is the other person's responsibility?

    b. Forego retribution.

    c. Pour out your anger in prayer or to a confidante.

2. Plan a constructive confrontation.

    a. Apologize, if appropriate.

    b. Use a soft, loving approach. Reflect on the fact that you need forgiveness as well.

    c. Be honest, yet tactful.

      d.   Indicate the behavior change needed.

3. Choose to forgive.

      a.   Release the other person from guilt and bondage.

      b.   Let go of the demands you want to make on the other person.

4. Return good to the offending party.

5. Change your attitude toward your spouse or the offending party.

Here is a question many people and writers ask:

Does Forgiveness = No Consequences? One thing I've been thinking about is: am I willing to treat a person who has hurt me as well as I would treat those I consider my closest friends (assuming that it's appropriate to interact with the person who hurt me)? It seems to me that until I am, I'm falling short of God's standards. Does it mean that there should be no consequences for the sin?

Answer: In his book, Total Forgiveness Kendall addresses the issue of how we treat others after they have let us down or mistreated us. There are consequences which sometimes can't be and shouldn't be removed when we forgive. He talks about how a woman forgave the person who raped her but, decided to testify in court in order to stop him from inflicting another crime.

In that case, judicial consequences were meted out along with forgiveness. He gives other examples as to how relationships are affected when someone mistreats or abuses us.

Here are some of my thoughts: You may decide that a friendship may change because that person cannot keep confidences. A change in relationship is not the same as forgiveness. You can let go of the blame and let go of any punishment and continuing to hold the wrong against a person—but, you may learn something about that person's character:

... that they can no longer be trusted with confidences or

... that they are not empathic and tend to be harsh when you divulge a weakness about yourself or

... that they are not responsible in keeping their commitments.

Therefore, you may forgive them, but, will no longer:

... become vulnerable and share your mistakes,

... share your problems with them,

... rely on or ask them to do a project with you, etc.

Forgiveness does not mean that you will:

... trust all people on the same level or

... expect all people to live up to certain standards or

... relinquish the consequences for their wrongful behavior.

On the one hand, you can give someone another chance to start over but, on the other hand, there are times when you will need to set boundaries.

Forgiveness doesn't equal trust! Forgiveness doesn't mean there won't be consequences for the person. Forgiveness does not mean that boundaries will remain the same.

Forgiveness will make you wiser. Forgiveness will challenge you at times to be vulnerable and to trust again. But, more importantly, forgiveness will set you free!

Foundational Insights:

Forgiveness sets you free from the prison of anger and resentment. Forgiveness ends the cycle of anger and blame moving you closer to reconciliation and new goals.

How to apologize if you have been rude, abrasive, curt, lied or shown negative anger toward someone else:

What can you do? First of all, take responsibility. Admit you were wrong and follow these simple steps by saying: "I'm sorry." "I was wrong." "Please forgive me."

It takes humility and self-awareness to confess your faults. In the long-run, you will grow as a person, become a better friend, spouse, co-worker or parent and work towards reconciliation.

Questions for Thought

1. Do the examples of Dith Pran and Mrs. Washington seem unrealistic, beyond your capability?

How were those two able to do the impossible and forgive their enemies?

2. Which of the "Steps to Forgiveness" seems the most difficult for you? Why?

What needs to happen to begin the process of forgiveness?

3. Which of the "Guidelines for Reconciliation and Forgiving" did you find the most encouraging or helpful? Why?

4. What steps can you take to apologize this week to someone you have hurt or disappointed? Write out what you will say. Example: I said/did _____ and think I have (hurt/disappointed)_____ you. I would like to apologize. Will you please forgive me?

10
WHEN TO TAKE
A BREAK

When angry, count to ten before you speak. If very angry, an hundred.
Thomas Jefferson

Speak when you are angry and you will make
the best speech you will ever regret.
Dr. Lawrence J. Peter

You may ask, "How do I know when to take a break (time-out)? Usually I am well into the fight or argument before I know what is happening, and I can't stop the escalation. I feel like I have no control."

Step 1 is recognition of what makes you easily frustrated. What are your triggers? Against which people and in what situations does your anger escalate? Go to the provocation scenario to find out. Maybe you already know you are easily frustrated by:

- someone's tone of voice,

- the use of certain demeaning or critical words,

- glaring looks,

- disregarding or disrespectful behavior,

- someone not listening to you,

- feeling overwhelmed or helpless.

Step 2 is to be ready to say you have to take a break from such situations as soon as they occur. Anger rears its ugly head in less than one second. That does not give you much time to prepare, analyze, and control yourself.

Now that you have determined the times, situations, and people that trigger your anger, follow these guidelines:

Take a deep breath. (This will help your body calm down some and will help clear your mind.)

Pray. (Many people have found this helpful.)

Tell the other person: "I have decided to take a break to consider the issue(s) or problem(s)." It's good to have a prepared statement since anger can keep you from thinking clearly. (Write it out in your own words on a card and keep it in your pocket or purse if that helps.) "I will get back to you by _____ ." (Give a reasonable time-frame.) If this is a spouse, then get back to him/her within thirty minutes to twenty-four hours.

Don't apologize for taking a break. Nehemiah did this, and so can you!

Move to another part of the house, do something to cool down, listen to soothing music, do relaxation exercises, take the dog for a walk, or go to the coffee room at work.

When you are taking your break—do the following:

- Evaluate the scenario between you and the other person.

- Decide what the issue is and what your concerns are.

- Determine what you want or need. What request can you make?

- How can you reconcile if this is necessary or possible?

- Review Handling Anger Effectively, the assertiveness and conflict chapters and apply the recommended steps to your situation.

- Determine if you are struggling with any cognitive distortions and challenge your thinking with reality and the truth.

Foundational Insights:

Taking a break is essential to interrupt the escalation of (physiological) anger and conflict, and to calm down. A time-out provides the opportunity to identify the issue, your perspective and thoughts, and to plan a healthy approach to manage the conflict.

Questions for Thought

1. How often does anger escalate beyond control in your life?

How have you tried to avoid or control this? Would taking time-outs help? Why or why not?

2. What triggers generally make your anger skyrocket?

3. Why do you find it so hard to take a break?

How do you feel (or how do you think you would feel) when you announce you need to take a break?

4. What effect has taking a time-out in the past had on your anger?

5. How will applying the time-out help you grow in managing your anger and behavior?

How motivated are you to apply this skill? (Circle one)

Very motivated. Moderately motivated.
Somewhat motivated. Not really motivated.

11
COGNITIVE
DISTORTIONS

Anger blows out the lamp of the mind.
Robert Green Ingersoll

Definitions

It is important to recognize how much thinking impacts your feelings and can trigger your anger. Circle which type of thinking is true of you. If you cannot evaluate your type of thinking, ask a confidante or close friend or family member to give you feedback.

Use the anger log sheet to evaluate examples of your thinking during angry scenarios. Compare and contrast it with this list to see where you might be struggling with cognitive distortions.

1. *All-or-nothing thinking:* You see things in black-and-white categories. If your performance is less than perfect, you consider yourself a total failure.

Give an example of how you may think this way. For example, "I always come-up short." "I am just a failure." "I can't handle this."

Do you feel like a total failure at times? Example: "I can never make it work."

Is this a distortion of the truth?

Do others tell you that you are not seeing things clearly?

How often does this thinking pattern occur?

☐ daily   ☐ weekly   ☐ more than once a day

☐ several times a day

With whom?

Where?

2. *Over-generalization:* You see one negative event as an unending pattern of defeat. Example: "We are always fighting" (even though this only happens once a week).

When do you think this way? What do you tell yourself?

How often does this thinking pattern occur?

☐ daily   ☐ weekly   ☐ more than once a day

☐ several times a day

With whom?

Where?

3. *Mental filter:* One negative detail or event is all you can dwell on. Thus you think that most of life is pretty negative as well. Do you always see the cup as half-empty? Example: "We would have had a great time at the picnic, but the mosquitoes almost ate us up!"

Do you dwell on the negative?

How often does this thinking pattern occur?

☐ daily ☐ weekly ☐ more than once a day

☐ several times a day

With whom?

Where?

4. *Disqualifying the positive:* You believe that positive experiences "don't count" for some reason or other. So you maintain a negative belief about your life even though circumstances contradict it.

Describe when this type of thinking occurs: Example: "Even though I got a good evaluation, I know my boss hates me."

☐ daily ☐ weekly ☐ more than once a day

☐ several times a day

With whom?

Where?

5. *Jumping to conclusions:* You automatically make a negative interpretation even though there are no definite facts that really support your conclusions.

How and when does this kind of thinking occur? Example:"My spouse came home late; he/she must be having an affair."

How often does this thinking pattern occur?

☐ daily ☐ weekly ☐ more than once a day

☐ several times a day

With whom?

Where?

a. *Mind-reading:* You indiscriminately conclude that someone is reacting negatively to you, and you don't bother to check it out. Example: "He/she went to lunch with another co-worker, so he/she must be mad at me."

When and how does this happen?

What do you tell yourself?

How often does this thinking pattern occur?

☐ daily ☐ weekly ☐ more than once a day

☐ several times a day

With whom?

Where?

b. *The fortune-teller error:* You anticipate that things will turn out badly, and you feel convinced that your prediction is an already-established fact. Example: "I know I'm going to fail this class" (even though you are getting good grades).

When and how does this happen? What do you tell yourself? How often does this thinking pattern occur?

☐ daily ☐ weekly ☐ more than once a day

☐ several times a day

With whom?

Where?

6. *Magnification (catastrophizing) or minimization:* You exaggerate the importance of things (such as your goof-up or someone else's achievement), or you inappropriately shrink things until they appear tiny (your own desirable qualities or the other person's imperfections). This is also called the "binocular trick."

When and how does this happen? What do you tell yourself? Example: "He always wins" (even though you won the chess game last week) or "my body is too fat" (even though you have been told you are the right weight).

How often does this thinking pattern occur?

☐ daily ☐ weekly ☐ more than once a day

☐ several times a day

With whom?

Where?

7. *Emotional reasoning:* You assume that your negative emotions necessarily reflect the way things really are: "I feel it; therefore it must be true."

When and how does this happen?

What do you tell yourself?

If you fall into this category, you are depending on your feelings as the measure of truth. How often does this thinking pattern occur?

☐ daily   ☐ weekly   ☐ more than once a day

☐ several times a day

With whom?

Where?

8. *"Should" statements:* You try to motivate yourself with "shoulds" and "shouldn'ts", as if you have to be whipped and punished before you can be expected to do anything. "Musts" and "oughts" are also offenders. The emotional consequence is guilt. When you direct should statements toward others, you feel anger, frustration, and resentment. Example: "I should clean the house in two hours." This is also a sign of perfectionism.

When and how does this happen?

What do you tell yourself?

How often does this thinking pattern occur?

☐ daily   ☐ weekly   ☐ more than once a day

☐ several times a day

With whom?

Where?

9. *Labeling and mislabeling:* This is an extreme form of over-generalization. Instead of describing your error, you attach a negative label to yourself. Example: "I'm a loser." When someone

else's behavior rubs you the wrong way, you attach a negative label to him or her: "She/he's a loser." Mislabeling involves describing an event with language that is highly colored and emotionally loaded.

When and how does this happen?

What do you tell yourself?

How often does this thinking pattern occur?

☐ daily   ☐ weekly   ☐ more than once a day

☐ several times a day

With whom?

Where?

10. *Personalization:* You see yourself as the cause of some negative external event that in fact you were not primarily responsible for.

When and how does this happen? Example: "If I had prayed more, my son wouldn't have had a car accident."

What do you tell yourself?

How often does this thinking pattern occur?

☐ daily   ☐ weekly   ☐ more than once a day

☐ several times a day
With whom?

Where?

This material has been adapted from Resource for Cognitive Distortions (revised) by D. Burns.

Foundational Insights:

Distorted and irrational thinking and expectations tend to escalate anger and conflict. When distorted thinking is challenged with reality and truth—effective anger management is possible.

Questions for Thought

1. Which of these cognitive distortions are you most vulnerable to? How does it or they affect your life (be as specific as you can)?

2. Why is it so easy to label (and to mislabel) ourselves and others? Why is this unhealthy or harmful?

3. Do you generally have a more distorted view of yourself or of others? Why? With what effects?

12
LOG YOUR THINKING

An angry man is again angry with himself
when he returns to reason.
Publilius Syrus

We encourage you to make a log of your thinking patterns as you use this course. Making a transition from unhealthy to healthy thinking is at times a difficult process but an important one.

Here is an example of faulty thinking:

"My friend showed up late for our dinner together. I concluded he/she really didn't want to be with me" (mind-reading).

What is the truth about this situation or person?

Describe the facts of the situation:

"Mary/Hank had a flat tire on the way to my house, which kept her/him from arriving on time. Therefore I should question the conclusion that she/he doesn't want to be with me. Maybe my low self-esteem is causing me to mind-read and jump to this negative conclusion."

We need to challenge such faulty thinking.

1. Give an example of a time when you used faulty thinking.

What is the truth about this situation or person?

Describe the facts of the situation:

Ways to challenge my faulty thinking:

2. Give another example of a time when you used faulty thinking.

What is the truth about this situation or person?

Describe the facts of the situation:

Ways to challenge my faulty thinking:

3. Give another example of a time when you used faulty thinking.

What is the truth about this situation or person?

Describe the facts of the situation:

Ways to challenge my faulty thinking:

Questions for Thought

1. What faulty thinking similarities do you see in the situations you have logged?

2. What will it take for you to believe the facts and truth versus your faulty thinking when you are confronted with anger-provoking situations?

13
PLAN TO CHANGE YOUR LIFE BY CHANGING YOUR THINKING

As you make such a plan and put it into action, the following questions and steps will be helpful:

1. What pattern of cognitive distortions do you see in your own life? Which distortions occur most often?

2. How can you challenge your thinking and bring about change?

3. This quote provides a challenge and a goal to aspire to: "Finally, whatever is true, whatever is honorable, whatever is just, whatever is pure, whatever is lovely, whatever is commendable, if there is any excellence, if there is anything worthy of praise, think about these things."[1]

What effect will thinking the best of others versus the worst have on you? Is it possible? Begin to challenge the negative thinking you have about yourself and others.

How has your negative thinking pattern affected you emotionally, mentally, and spiritually—maybe even physically?

4. What can you do to begin changing your faulty thinking?

Examples: Make a log of your faulty thinking patterns, and challenge them with the truth.

Read inspirational resources daily, pray often.

Talk with a confidante, counselor, pastor, and advisor.

5. How can you begin to think about whatever is true, noble, right, pure, lovely, admirable, and excellent?

How will thinking like this affect your life?

Will you be less depressed? Less anxious? More optimistic? More hopeful?

6. Do you really want to get better? What would your life be like if you were more hopeful and optimistic?

Questions for Thought

1. Have you tried such a plan before? Did it work? Why or why not?

2. Which of these steps do you think will be the hardest? Why? What might make this step a little easier to implement?

3. How do you feel about the question, "Do you really want to get better?" Be honest. Why do you think this question is either fair or unfair? Helpful or irritating?

14
HOW EMOTIONAL INTELLIGENCE IMPACTS ANGER

The ability to understand and regulate emotions as well as understand the emotions of others and handle relationships constructively = emotional intelligence.

Emotional Intelligence Skills Help You Manage Anger

What does emotional intelligence have to do with managing anger? Maybe you are wondering, "Why should I learn about emotional intelligence? If I am keeping my anger in check, that should be enough."

Experts have discovered that people with a high degree of emotional intelligence (EI) are more motivated to manage their anger, get better results, and build healthy relationships. Wouldn't you like to experience the kind of life where anger no longer dominates you but becomes one of the tools you use to achieve your goals and experience a more satisfying life?

Let's first take a look at the meaning of EI. Daniel Goleman writes, "Emotional intelligence is the ability to recognize your own feelings and those of others, motivate yourself, manage your emotions well and in your relationships."

Growing in anger management skills is helpful. But developing EI will improve your life in greater ways. How? Ari Novak, Ph.D., LMFT, a leader in Anger Management, attests to the importance of EI in managing anger. He states, "After treating clients with anger-related issues for over 7 years, I have come to realize that increasing skills in Emotional Intelligence (EI) is one of the most effective interventions a person can learn. EI skills improve performance in so many areas of life including leadership, intimate relationships, and simple day to day situations." You will gain control of your anger to further higher purposes in life, from opening up doors on your career path to building satisfying relationships.

How Emotional Intelligence Works

When you develop Emotional Intelligence you become adept at the following:

1. Self-awareness. Self-awareness is having the ability to identify your own emotions, strengths, and weaknesses. This foundational step in EI provides the ability to monitor your feelings and determine what triggers your anger. People who lack self-awareness of feelings are more prone to becoming ensnared by them and being left at their mercy. By gaining the skills to watch carefully and oversee your feelings, particularly your anger, you will be able to identify what the issues are and make better decisions about responding to difficult situations. Find out how you are doing in the area of self-awareness by reviewing the "Anger Survey," "Power of Anger," and "Managing Stress" chapters.

2. Self-management. Self-management is the ability to effectively be in control of your motives and regulate your behavior. Self-management is built on self-awareness and provides the capacity for bouncing back from failure or disappointments. By gaining the ability to apply the cognitive and behavioral skills found in this book, you will become more proficient at controlling unhealthy anger and emotions and building effective skills to guide anger into assertiveness, problem-solving, forgiveness, time-outs, and healthy self-talk. Examine the chapters covering these skills and determine your level of progress in applying them.

3. Self-motivation. Self-motivation is monitoring and controlling one's emotions in order to achieve goals. This ability delays immediate and temporary gratification by stifling impulsiveness in order to accomplish projects and long-term objectives. When you see the bigger picture of reaping the consequences for your actions, you will be self-motivated to redirect your anger and emotions into healthy communication and behavioral skills. The concept of this book is that "you can have good anger." That idea has motivated many people to change. Go back to the "When Anger is Good" chapter. Ask yourself, "What consequences have I experienced from unhealthy anger? What are the pros for expressing my anger in healthy ways? How does this motivate me to change?"

4. Social awareness. Social awareness is gaining empathy for other people. Empathy is the capacity to understand what others are saying and feeling and why they feel and act as they do. Empathy is built on self-awareness, self-management, and self-motivation. When you are able to empathize, you will put yourself in other people's shoes, understand their feelings and viewpoints, and consider their needs. Review the "Managing Conflict" chapter. How have you applied the Sum-Up skill? What has been the result? Read the rest of this chapter to really learn the importance of and how to apply empathy.

5. Relationship development. Relationship development is the capacity to act in such a way that you are able to influence others without controlling them. This allows you to achieve personal and relational goals. When you employ assertiveness and empathy skills and negotiate issues while considering the best interests of all parties, you will develop healthy and compatible relationships with others. Your relationships will improve when you cultivate assertiveness, empathy, and conflict management skills (see the EI competencies list by Daniel Goleman and Hay Group).

This book is geared to help you develop in the areas of self-awareness and self-management by understanding and managing anger, one of the most stressful and overwhelming emotions. You can learn anger's underlying causes and triggers and redirect it into healthy thinking, skills and behavior.

Dr. Pfeiffer writes, "The development of Emotional Intelligence initially means to recognize—actually feel—the sensations of frustration, annoyance, and anger in your body. Maybe you feel these in the form of tension in your chest, or you notice your face getting warm or red, maybe your hands are beginning to sweat. Once you are familiar and aware of these bodily sensations you are now ready to begin talking about your emotions as you actually experience them. The process of recognizing, experiencing and talking about your emotions puts you on the road to understanding and having compassion for yourself and then the ability to understand that others also have emotions too . . . you now have the capacity for empathy."

The Next Step: Learning to Empathize With Others

In order to really develop EI, we encourage you to focus on how to be a more empathic person as this is the key to social awareness and is critical to relationship compatibility.

First, take the empathy inventory found in the Appendix of this book. Afterward come back and finish reading the remainder of this chapter in order to identify the importance of developing empathy.

What is empathy?

Empathy is authentically listening to and understanding someone else's point of view. It's about seeing the situation from the other person's perspective. Empathy requires the ability to identify feelings and care about other people enough to consider their opinions and views, even when theirs differ from your own. Empathy will help decrease your frustration and anger-triggers because you will be focused on thinking about the other person's needs and not just your own.

Why is empathy important?

Empathy is the key to social awareness and is thus a key for defusing anger. By exploring someone else's viewpoint and feelings and putting yourself in the other person's shoes, you will be more likely to give the other person the benefit of the doubt and less likely to hold on to anger and resentment.

Gaining skills of listening to others and empathizing with them are essential for building relationships, defusing conflict and anger, and truly connecting with other people. It can build your relationships with those you interact with at your job such as customers, clients, and coworkers. It can also help bond, bridge, and mend personal relationships with spouses, family members, and friends.

Most of us spend 70% of the day communicating. With nearly three-quarters of our day spent communicating, you would think that listening would compose half of that communication. Yet only 45% of our time communicating with others is actually spent listening. Statistics show that spouses communicate only 10-20 minutes per day.

Listening and empathy skills are foundational to interpersonal communication, and yet surprisingly we are rarely taught these skills in the classroom or from our parents.

It is insulting to be ignored, interrupted, or neglected. We all want to be heard and understood. We want others to really care and understand our feelings and opinions. We want to know we matter. We want validation. And yet we have difficulty giving to others the very thing we want from them.

How is empathy expressed?

One of the best ways to validate and connect with others is to ask them questions about themselves and to really listen to their response. This "active listening" is briefly discussed in the chapter on "Managing Conflict."

People love to talk about themselves. Write out some questions in advance of meeting with people that you can ask to help you find out more about who they are and what their lives are like. Then be prepared to genuinely listen. After they have shared, paraphrase what they have said. If you can paraphrase and summarize what someone has said to you, you will send the message that you were listening, you understand and care for that person. Listening and paraphrasing is one of the most effective and important ways to validate someone. Taking the time to understand someone and enter into their world is the first step to becoming an empathetic person.

Empathy goes the extra mile. It listens with the heart. It cares about and identifies with another person's needs, opinions, and feelings. Empathy, when acted out, listens intently and actively by asking clarifying questions and reflecting back what the person has said in a kind and considerate way. Empathy doesn't mean you have to agree with the other person. Empathy genuinely tries to understand what the other person is saying and what comprises that person's situation and needs. Try to imagine what it's like to be in that person's situation or take a walk in their shoes. We all know what it means to really listen. Listening is more than hearing and processing words. Listening understands, affirms, and accepts the other person's meaning, experience, and feelings.

Here are some benefits from practicing good listening and empathy skills:

- You are able to care for and understand the other person. Often the conversation is directed toward emotional issues that are very important to others. As a result, people will enjoy talking to you and will open up more.

- Even if you misunderstand others, you allow them to correct your interpretations. As a consequence, you are able to grow and learn more about other people.

- You let the speaker know that you, the listener, accept the speaker. In return the other person will feel more comfortable telling his or her story and feelings to you. Since the speaker feels safe to talk about personal subjects with you, he or she will be more vulnerable by expressing his or her deeper emotions, exploring his or her emotions and problem-solving.

- It decreases any frustration or anger you may have.

- It can also promote forgiveness because we gain a greater understanding of the other person's experience.

- It can prevent or reduce negative assumptions about others because empathy helps us build understanding of the other person.

- It fosters meaningful, helpful, and close friendships.

You may be thinking that this is too much. You have enough problems and concerns of your own. You don't have the time or desire to concern yourself with other people and their needs. Or maybe you feel angry that no one has shown empathy to you and so you do not wish to show empathy to others. Perhaps you just want to "live your life" and not be bothered with learning and practicing empathy skills. But there's something in it for you, too. When you are empathetic with others, they are more likely to show empathy toward you. And as you practice empathy, you too will benefit from your actions as you will be on your way to liberating yourself from the negative patterns of bitterness and anger.

We believe that when you build your emotional intelligence skills, you will discover a greater ability to manage your anger, get better results, and experience healthy relationships. Challenge yourself to really grow by writing out and applying the following questions and assignments. Then you will discover the kind of life where anger no longer controls you but becomes one of the tools you use to achieve your goals and experience a more fulfilling life.

Foundational Insights: Developing empathy is key to promoting deeper connection and understanding between people and integral to becoming an emotionally intelligent person. Empathy provides awareness and sensitivity for the other person's point of view and experiences—thus defusing anger, cognitive distortions, and conflict. Empathy considers the best interests of others.

Questions for Thought

1. Write out 2-3 sentences that describe your understanding of emotional intelligence.

2. How can developing EI help you achieve your goals in your life and in your relationships? How might developing EI impact your home or work situation?

3. What is your opinion on the importance of empathy? How can empathy have an impact on your anger?

4. Circle your final score on the empathy inventory found in the appendix of the book: Empathy rating: poor = 1-4; moderate = 5-10; high = 11-14.

5. From the Empathy Inventory provide recent examples of the "B" statements you checked on a separate sheet.

6. On a scale from 1-10 (1 being the lowest and 10 the highest) how motivated are you to develop empathy skills? Share your reasons for being motivated or unmotivated.

7. How will supportive, empathic communication change your relationships?

8. Write out and practice the paraphrasing skills found in the "Assertiveness" chapter this week.

9. In order to determine your growth in self-awareness, self-management, and self-motivation, complete the following questions:

   a. From the survey in chapter 1 which kinds of people and situations generally trigger your frustration and anger?

   b. How do you normally try to calm yourself down? What phrases or thoughts help defuse your anger?

   c. What skills from the book do you regularly apply to stressful situations that trigger anger or frustration?

   Assertiveness: _____

Empathy: _____

Time-Out: _____

Problem-Solving: _____

Changing Self-Talk or Cognitive Distortions: _____

Forgiveness: _____

Stress Management and Relaxation: _____

Prayer: _____

d. What motivates you to develop EI? Rate your motivation level here:

Low (1-3):____ Moderate (4-6):____High (7-10):____

10. In order to determine your growth in social awareness, empathy, and constructive relationships, complete the following questions:

a. Take the empathy inventory again in the appendix and rate yourself: _____

b. What skills are you applying to manage conflict and work through relationship misunderstandings?

Paraphrasing, Sum-Up: _____

Active listening: _____

Time-out: _____

Assertiveness: _____

Problem-solving: _____

Forgiveness: _____

c. What steps will you take this week to grow in empathy skills?

d. Which skills from the conflict chapter will help you develop healthier relationships?

e. How will forgiveness play a part in enhancing your relationships?

f. How can you apply the apology steps to relationships?

15
DEALING WITH RAGE

Get rid of all bitterness, rage and anger,
brawling and slander, along with every form of malice.
Ephesians 4:31

What is the difference between Anger and Rage?

Anger is a common emotion that we all experience from time to time. Frustration or a lack of patience can lead to anger. You may be at your wits end with your boss, your co-worker, or your husband. You can feel the anger building up when your boss asks you to meet an impossible deadline, or when your colleague takes the credit for your hard work in the weekly sales meeting.

You get furious when your spouse leaves their clothes in a heap on the bathroom floor, or forgets to clean up after dinner or take the trash out for the fifth time this week. You respond by yelling, pouting or slamming a door. Anger is an emotion that can be controlled. If you have trouble controlling your anger or find yourself getting angry more frequently get professional help. Anger management sessions can help you maintain control before your anger turns to rage.

What is Rage?

Rage occurs when anger escalates out of control. Rage results in violence, destruction and can often be a senseless act of desperation.

This extremely dangerous reaction to frustration, perceived pain, or feeling threatened is not normal. Rage is an aggressive, explosive behavior that can lead to incarceration, self- destruction or even death. Incidents of rage often cause damage to others and property. When a person is experiencing a period of rage, he/she cannot think clearly, or consider the consequences of his/her actions.

Controlling the Rage Within

I recently received this question: When I get angry, I blow up so fast that I don't have time to stop and think or ask for God's wisdom. I know all of these things would help, but by the time I think of it I've already done the damage. What can I do to help get control of my temper and the rage within? Signed, Anonymous.

Many people have felt this way. Anger is often a primary emotion which quickly triggers the brain within $1/20^{th}$ of a second. We often are primed to get angry because we are experiencing low self-worth, disrespect, unmet goals, disappointments, abuse, expectations, fears, sin, selfishness, skill deficits, stress, PTSD, and other emotional or relationship problems.

So, what Happens? You encounter a rude family member or a co-worker who is pestering you to hurry up with your part of a project – and your anger immediately rears its head in less than a second-- increasing your heart rate and breathing – and all you want to do is loudly let him/her know how disrespectful they are. Instead, you might hold your anger inside and then, blow-up later on when you get home. Or you may decide to just ignore the person. Of course, these options won't solve the issue and your anger will keep brewing.

The question is: how can you prevent such an overpowering emotional response and how can you respond in a healthy way to these kinds of triggering events?

Take the following steps:

1. Write out and log recent times of anger. Explore what happened, what the issue was, how you felt and what resulted.

2. Then write out times in the past when you were able to control your anger and prevent an outburst. Maybe it occurred at work or school or at a community event.

How did you control it? What did you do or say?

What did you tell yourself to calm down? Most people tend to be able to control their anger and prevent rage at times thus proving that they can have control over it.

Identify your triggers and when you are first feeling annoyed, frustrated, irritated. What does it feel like in your body? Where are you feeling tense? Is you breathing shallow or fast? What were you thinking prior to the situation? Were you already stressed out and irritated?

Learn to take a break (time-outs) immediately. You can walk away from situations/people that trigger your anger. Tell him/her that you will get back to them in an hour or two. Give yourself time to cool off: 10-30 min. Take a walk, pray and do something calming like diaphragmatic breathing or a relaxation exercise.

Explore: Get your thinking part of the brain engaged by asking:

What is the real issue? Ask yourself -- what are my feelings underneath my anger? If you let go of the anger – do you feel like you are losing control? How can you control yourself instead of others? Apply the Thinking Ahead Reminders when you encounter a triggering situation. Is there a request you can make? How can you negotiate or compromise some conflict you are having?

Avoid lots of caffeine. Completely avoid alcohol and drugs, unless you are taking a doctor's prescription. Caffeine increases the metabolism, heart rate and blood pressure, and causes mood irritability. Alcohol and drugs may give a person a "high" or mellow feeling at first and will seem to relieve stress but the effects are temporary and soon after you will actually feel more irritable and depressed and angry feelings will not only return but usually escalate.

What else is going on? You may be dealing with a lot of stress or loss. This needs to be explored and worked through possibly with the help of a counselor. Explore how you can decrease stress in your life.

Begin an exercise program so that you can work off some of the stress in your life physically. Learn to pray, read the Psalms and seek the Lord.

Learning to communicate assertively is one of the most important tools for expressing your anger in a healthy way. Share more openly and lovingly your needs, requests and opinions with others. Start setting boundaries so that you are not taking on other people's responsibilities. Review the chapter on Assertiveness. Depression can play a part in anger or vice versa. I would encourage you to go to counseling and see a psychiatrist for an evaluation and diagnosis and any recommended medication.

Rage Questionnaire © copyright 2021 by Lynette J. Hoy, NCC, LCPC, CAMS-V

How would you describe rage? Check all the statements that you think characterize rage.

1. Losing control of emotions and behavior resulting in harm:
   _____

2. Intentional behavior that causes damage to something or someone:_____

3. Violent, uncontrolled anger:_____

4. Explosive anger:_____

I fly off the handle (into a rage): Check which behavior applies to you.

A. By yelling, screaming, ___

B. With hurtful/abusive remarks, ___

C. By threatening, ___

D. By throwing things, ___

E. By hitting or damaging something, ___

F. By hitting or damaging someone, ___

G. By swearing, cursing at someone, ___

H. Describe: _____

Note: if you are dealing with any of the above behaviors—you have a rage problem. Seek a mental health evaluation and counseling.

I have expressed the above behavior:

How often?	2-5 x Daily	Once Daily	Weekly	Monthly
1. At the slightest disruption	_____	_____	_____	_____
2. During a disagreement	_____	_____	_____	_____
3. Because of a disappointment	_____	_____	_____	_____
4. At a negative remark	_____	_____	_____	_____
5. Something blocks my goals	_____	_____	_____	_____
6. When someone is rude	_____	_____	_____	_____
7. Someone is disrespectful	_____	_____	_____	_____
8. When a car cuts me off on the highway	_____	_____	_____	_____
9. Because of loud noises	_____	_____	_____	_____
10. During too much stress	_____	_____	_____	_____
11. During conflict at work	_____	_____	_____	_____
12. With my spouse/partner	_____	_____	_____	_____
13. With my boss	_____	_____	_____	_____
14. With my children	_____	_____	_____	_____
15. With certain family members	_____	_____	_____	_____
16. With some friends	_____	_____	_____	_____

17. Other: (describe situation, trigger) _____

_____

18. Never expressed rage: _____

19. I have had thoughts about hurting or harming someone else or damaging their property but never acted on it.

Circle one: Often   sometimes   rarely   never

How I feel just prior to the explosive outburst or rageful event: Circle all that apply

1.   Like my head is going to explode:

2.   A tingling in my fingers or spine

3. Fearful

4. Stressed-out

5. Incensed

6. Indignant

7. Not applicable

8. Other:_____

Evaluate your rage assessment. Now, complete the following:

Describe a recent situation when you expressed rage?

What happened? What triggered the rage?

What were you thinking?

What did your rage look like?

What were the consequences?

When have you been able to control or prevent rage?

What occurred to help you manage or prevent the rage?

What does rage feel like for you?

When is it ok to express rage?

What happens during road rage?

Here's a writer who discusses road rage:

"When some idiot cuts me off and almost cause an accident.... The anger flows to the surface, in words you cannot print, and I want to retaliate-cut him off, rude gesture, yell inside the car. I think back to my misspent youth when I would follow a guy like that, wait for a traffic stop, and pull him out of the care to "educate him in proper driving etiquette". Someone else said, "I never really get angry unless I'm driving and someone cuts me off. Then, I really get angry."

What is really happening when people get behind the wheel of a car and experience a road rage tirade? Why does it happen to some people and not to others?

When you get in the driving seat of your car - you gain a sense of power and control. As you proceed into traffic - you become aware of stressors - stressors which conflict with your sense of power and control. You will have an automatic response to the stress and the potential loss of power and control. Your fight/flight mechanism will kick in causing an immediate physiological reaction, i.e., triggering the emotional center of the brain (amygdala) in less than a second. If you are on-edge from other stressors or if you struggle with "hot self-talk" thinking derogatory remarks such as "that idiot" or vengeful statements such as: "I'm going to show him a thing or two"- you will act these out. You will follow the guy wanting to pull him out of the car to educate him in proper driving etiquette.

Ironically, when you try to "educate the guy in driving etiquette" - you become rude, obnoxious and harassing.

People who easily succumb to the stress and pressures of everyday life are taking out their aggressions on the road. The anonymity of a safe, protected car allows drivers from all walks of life to take out their aggression on the guy traveling at 50 M.P.H. in the fast lane.

There is no formal profile of the typical road rage driver. Gender, age, race, and economic situation do not factor into the road rage equation. Once behind the wheel, drivers feel a certain sense of security. There is a certain sense of power and an enormous sense of personal space and safety we obtain from driving a car.

Americans have a love affair with the automobile. Since the first Fords rolled off the assembly line a sense of prestige and security has been drawn from car ownership. Through society, films, and television Americans learn from a very young age that freedom comes from sitting behind the wheel of a car. The sense of freedom, security, and power which comes from being an anonymous driver in an equally anonymous crowd is what fuels the fire of road rage. These feelings allow some to justify their aggressive acts and behaviors toward other drivers. The good news is that these feelings and behaviors are basically learned and can be changed. Many states are now exploring and adopting programs in order to combat road rage.

What do experts say are the best ways to combat road rage? Learn to counter overall stress, anxiety, frustration and tension on a daily basis.

Learn some basic relaxation skills to counter a highly-inflammable fight/flight response. For some people - applying faith, prayer, reading scriptures and meditating is very helpful. Most importantly, change your thinking and attitude. If you generally have a problem with "hot self-talk", a self-righteous attitude or a belief that you must be in control - you will succumb to road rage and other kinds of rage.

Questions About Road Rage. Circle the statements that apply to you:

1. I tailgate another driver to encourage them to speed up and go faster.

2. I flash my lights in order to signal other drivers to move right.

3. I use obscene gestures with other drivers.

4. I signal my lane changes.

5. I use my horn to indicate my irritation with other drivers.

6. I frequently change lanes to the left and the right to get past slower traffic.

7. If someone cuts me off I will try to return the favor.

8. I normally drive the speed of the traffic as long as it is moving sufficiently.

9. I try not to make eye contact with angry drivers.

10. I try to be a polite and courteous driver.

11. I stay right except to pass.

12. I drive the speed of the traffic.

13. I don't exceed the speed limit.

14. I get into confrontations with other drivers.

15. I follow all motor vehicle laws.

16. I feel that all other drivers are complete idiots.

17. When there is a conflict between me and another driver, I am never the one who is at fault.

18. I feel angry when another motorist does something stupid.

19. I think that it is important to drive to the speed of the traffic.

20. I think that most accidents are caused by drivers less experienced than me.

21. I try to avoid driving behaviors that may irritate or antagonize others.

22. If someone lets me into their lane, I will wave at them (or flash my lights) to acknowledge their kindness.

23. I will avoid driving in another's "blind spot".

24. I think that most drivers who pass me are "going way too fast".

25. Slow drivers don't bother me, I just go around them.

26. I am surely the best driver on the road.

27. I only pass people who are going significantly slower than me.

28. If I see someone "flipping me off" I will return the gesture.

29. I think that there are a lot of slow drivers on the road.

30. I will leave a space in front of my vehicle in order to let other drivers merge right, into my lane.

OK, now consider the fact that you have a road rage problem if you circled any of these statements:

1, 3, 5, 6, 7, 14, 16, 28

If you circled any of these statements – you may be at risk of road rage:

2, 17, 18, 20, 24, 26, 29

Driving involves three domains: affect (our feelings), cognition (how we think), and behavior (how we behave). To begin a driving personality make-over requires the conscious evaluations of all these three domains. It requires recognizing our feelings, thoughts and behaviors while driving; identifying a behavior to be modified; taking the necessary steps to modify the behavior; taking the responsibility for our actions; and then applying the modified behavior into our driving.

Here are some insights about anger and rage:

1. *We need to take responsibility* for our thoughts, actions and personal change. We need to be compassionate change-agents in an unstable world.

We need to get help if our anger crosses the line to seething rage.

There are many people who have expressed rage and some have verbalized thoughts of killing others. This is very troubling. Why? Because what people think about – they will likely act out. Venting thoughts of harming others is threatening, evil and dangerous!

2. *We need to have a comprehensive view of rage and violence.* The roots emanate from sin, selfishness and evil in our lives. There are other reasons such as psychological or personality disorders which play a part - but, the acts of rage and violence are ultimately a choice. We choose to act out rageful thoughts, out-of-control anger and revenge.

3. *Identify when to help others and how to protect ourselves*: We cannot take lightly what people say and do. We cannot minimize what we think, say and do. We need to recognize when people around us are deteriorating, explore how to help and intervene. We need to report when their behavior becomes threatening.

4. *Can anger management help?* Yes! Anger management is educational and provides strategies and skills for people who are mentally capable of change and willing to change. Anger management can help people *prevent rage,* change their thinking, self-talk, behavior, and communication and learn to develop empathy and forgiveness.

5. *If you are quietly seething with rage - you can take steps towards change.* You can learn how to express your feelings in ways that are appropriate and helpful.

Plan to change by:

- Knowing and reducing your triggers.
- Taking time-outs and thinking about healthy solutions.
- Learning diaphragmatic breathing and relaxation skills
- Reducing and managing stress
- Changing your brain and the way you think: challenging false beliefs, cognitive distortions
- Applying the "Thinking Ahead Reminders"

If you or someone else is dealing with abusive behaviors, mental health or personality disorders, psychosis, addiction issues, severe developmental disabilities or out-of-control rage, seek counseling. See www.nbcc.org for a referral.

Rage can often become violent and harmful. But, you can learn to deal with rage in a healthy way.

16
SUMMARY

The world needs anger. The world often continues
to allow evil because it isn't angry enough.
Bede Jarrett

We have designed What's Good About Anger? to help you discover how to transform your anger into a positive force. You most likely identified several sources and triggers for the anger you have been experiencing and were comforted to know that even righteous men like Nehemiah felt "very angry."

The central point of this book demonstrates the importance of managing stress and triggers in order to de-escalate anger and prevent a harmful reaction. Taking time to reflect on the issues and how to approach the person or situation will help guide you toward a healthy rather than a hostile or cold-shoulder response.

Learning how to communicate assertively by "speaking the truth in love" is a healthy way to direct your anger and frustration.

Nehemiah's example in taking a time-out, confronting, and problem-solving demonstrates how to use your anger to motivate and change an unjust situation. Corrie ten Boom's, Dith Pran's and Mrs. Washington's stories illustrate that it is possible to transform anger into forgiveness even towards evil perpetrators. On the other hand, forgiveness does not always mean that consequences will be eliminated.

Challenge yourself with these final questions:

- When have you handled your anger effectively? What made the difference?

- How can you begin applying a time-out when your anger begins to rear its ugly head?

- How can you better evaluate the legitimacy of the issues and triggers underlying your angry feelings?

- How can you communicate your needs more assertively and implement the conflict resolution skills?

- When did you forgive an offender?

- How does your thinking need to change in order to see people and life truthfully rather than through the eyes of anger?

- How has developing emotional intelligence impacted your anger and relationships?

You can change. You can grow out of harmful anger, the kind of rage or hidden anger that blocks the peace in your life.

Continue to log your anger and responses. Challenge yourself to grow in healthy living and responses to anger and stress.

You can choose to be angry or not. You have the power to express anger in healthy or unhealthy ways. Your response to anger will help you grow or make you miserable.

Maybe you have found that you need something more to help manage your anger. Consider discovering how God can provide you with supernatural strength to manage your emotions and give you guidance for living. Read the articles and resources found at:

www.counselcareconnection.org and www.whatsgoodaboutanger.com

We invite you to read the FAQs (frequently asked questions) about anger in the next section. We hope that you will find various individuals' inquiries and our brief answers helpful. We wish you success in your quest to conquer anger!

FAQS
Frequently Asked Questions
About Anger

The following FAQs have been selected and adapted from real e-mails posted on the CounselCare Connection and the All About Anger blog, a counseling service of Lynette Hoy. You may want to read all these FAQs and answers, or just select those that relate most closely to your own anger struggles.

Question — Boyfriend's Anger: My boyfriend is the kindest, sweetest guy on the planet most of the time, but in the last couple of years he has hit me a few times. I have a nasty mouth, as he has, and this I guess hasn't helped him. I have learned to try to calm the situation somewhat when I feel things are getting out of control. If he starts raising his voice, I shut up like a clam and hope for it to pass. It always does, and he apologizes afterward. He had a very traumatic upbringing. He was violent for many years when he was younger but for many years now hasn't hurt a fly as far as I know, until he met me. For the last few months nothing happened; we had rows, but it never turned violent. But then we had a recent incident in which I took a hit to the arm which was quite nasty. I didn't retaliate but told him off and asked him never to do that again. I calmly explained that I will not tolerate that sort of behavior. I have never been a violent person by nature and had vowed some time ago that showing my aggression back was wrong, totally not me, and

I had to learn when to walk away. We have had confrontations in the past and at times this man, I'm ashamed to say, has driven me to hit back. What worries me with the recent incident is that he has showed no remorse for it this time, even after I had to get it looked at, making some excuse to the doctor. He said I should have kept my mouth shut. I think he is trying to make light of it, and although he did apologize in a way, I worry at times that his path to his previous violence is opening up again. This incident seemed less aggressive than the others in that at least I didn't get a smack across the face. I'm not making light of it, but I'm so disappointed in him that once again he lashed out. I'm also feeling disappointed in myself that while I know that I can say the most hurtful things, it's now come to the point where I'm modifying my behavior when he has an angry mood. I love this man. I think he may be willing to go to couples' therapy, even though he wasn't willing to continue to see the therapist for his own issues. Is this a place to start? Is something better than nothing? I do believe things are getting better.

Answer — My advice is to get out of this relationship now! This man is a batterer. You will not change him. As you have seen, the battering is escalating. I believe people can change, but he demonstrates no remorse and this is a very bad sign. Most likely the battering and abuse will escalate. You are putting yourself in danger by staying in this relationship.

Ask yourself: "how healthy is it for me to take responsibility to calm the situation down? How can I build trust in a relationship where I can't feel safe and am experiencing fear?" Don't try and talk yourself into staying in the relationship, and don't let him talk you into it. Look at the facts. The abuse is escalating, and he has a history of violence. It will only get worse.

The Good Book says, "the Lord hates violence." God wants you to live peacefully and not to put yourself in danger or associate with someone who is hot-tempered. See the www.saferelationships.net site for domestic abuse resources.

Question — Anger Explosions and Drinking: I guess it is time for me to admit, I may have a problem with anger. But my anger is strange. I just tend to get so upset when someone is mad at me, and I take it out on them and myself. Scenario: AR gets mad at me for not doing dishes, so I get upset that she is mad at me and just keep it bottled up until I explode (which is usually fueled by drinking). I do not physically harm her, nor would I ever touch a girl in that way, but I can become a complete jerk and use sarcasm to make her feel as small as a mouse. What I want to know is, how can I help suppress this type of anger? Should I see a counselor?

Answer — You stated that you keep your anger bottled up and then explode—usually after drinking. Alcohol is a trigger for anger since it lowers inhibitions and the ability to control your behavior. It also increases irritability, and distorts your thinking.

Recommendations: I suggest you cut down on or better yet, stop the drinking since you are concerned about your relationship and not destroying your marriage.

Also, when you begin to feel tense and don't agree with your wife, learn how to express your feelings in an assertive way. When you bottle up your feelings—they will build and then erupt.

When you express your feelings right away—for example, "I feel upset when you say _____ ; I will take care of the dishes after this show"—you are more likely to resolve the issue and/or begin problem-solving in a healthy way.

Take a time-out when you feel the anger rising within. Begin to recognize the triggers for anger. During your time-out you can think through the issue and how to communicate your needs or requests respectfully.

Question — Is anger right or wrong? After reading your book and thinking about some of the concepts, I have to let you know that I have a little different opinion on the emotion of anger. I think anger is just an emotion like all other emotions. They are God-given and are flags that guide us to think about our irrational thoughts and actions. Anger is neither right nor wrong. What is right or wrong is our response to our anger. We can choose to hurt ourselves, others, God, and things or we can choose to respond appropriately and solve the problem with truth and righteousness. Our irrational thinking or cognitive distortions and acting on them are wrong. I believe that our anger response is just a signal to other underlying problems. Anger itself is not the culprit.

Answer — The actual feeling of anger may not in itself be wrong. Often the emotion is wrought out of negative thoughts or may lead to sin by becoming resentful, punitive, and envious or acting in a harmful, destructive way.

The truth is that anger is a choice. When you perceive an event or thought as threatening—your fight/flight response is activated. You quickly turn the feelings or cognitive perception of hurt, fear, sadness, loneliness, anxiety into anger in order to gain a sense of control. Anger may be the emotion you recognize first.

Here's an important question to ask: Is all anger wrong? No. Many times we become angry at injustice as Nehemiah did. We should be angry when someone burglarizes the home of our neighbor, terrorizes the country or makes false accusations against us. Many times someone has offended or taken advantage of us injuring our dignity or reputation. Anger in those cases is good, normal and healthy. When you process good anger, you will act it out in a healthy, respectful way towards others.

Question — Getting mad over things that don't matter: Why do we get so mad over things that don't really matter, like getting cut off in traffic by someone who's in too much of a hurry?

Answer — Maybe it's cumulative stress. Or maybe it has to do with putting up with rude people throughout the day and feeling disrespected over and over again. Each of us has a limit as to the amount of stress we can take. Each of us has a limit on the amount of disrespect or abuse thrown our way.

Our perspective and thinking really does cause the anger though. People have said to me, "I don't choose to be angry. Anger just happens to me." I disagree. Look back at situations when you became angry. Maybe you were angry at your spouse for disagreeing with you about how to discipline the children. What was underneath the anger? Was his/her disagreement with you really that bad? Or was the issue that you felt disregarded or that your opinion didn't matter and thus you thought he/she didn't really care about you? This kind of thinking is mind-reading and personalization—cognitive distortions that cause angry reactions. Doesn't your spouse have a right to disagree with you?

You have disagreed with your spouse in the past over issues and plans. Did that mean that you were disregarding his/her opinion and didn't care about him/her? Probably not. Spouses should disagree with each other at times. Spouses should not act like clones. It's healthy to disagree. It's not healthy to mind-read.

If your mind tends to judge others quickly, thinking the worst about someone's actions or words, you will be easily angered. On the other hand, if you train your mind to think the best about someone and give them the benefit of the doubt about situations, you will find yourself less frustrated and angry. This kind of reaction or response comes more easily when you seek help from your Higher Power.

Question — Taking anger out on myself: I need some help. You see, I am nineteen years old . . . and sure, I've been through a lot, but that's life right? Well, my father was a very violent man . . . in turn my brother is. The thing about me, though, is that I am incredibly angry and violent toward myself. Any little thing goes wrong and I freak out. (I was a cutter for years, but I am talking more about beating myself.) I tend to be incredibly edgy with others when I am in this state, and I snap back at them. I would never hurt them. But I am doing that in the sense of their psychological stress from having to deal with me. I just can't believe some of the stupid things I do or say.

I am incredibly disappointed in myself and wish myself to change. But it all seems so overwhelming. I have been questioned about the bruises I have on my body (mostly from pushing myself into walls, purposely falling down stairs, punching myself—all forms of punishment). Being nineteen, I can usually find something else to blame it on. I want people to see the girl that is somewhere inside of me—the one that is pretty cool—if she even still exists. I'm just hoping to find a way to deal with this. I have never seen a counselor, basically because I cannot afford it, and the other reason is because I don't think I am far-gone enough to see one. So, any advice?

Answer — It's obvious that you are hurting very badly inside. Your emotional distress has caused you to take out your anger, rage, grief, helplessness, hopelessness, resentment, hurt, inner pain, and unfulfilled needs on yourself. Someone else suffering with similar issues wrote: "I self-injure because I have so much pain and anger built up inside and I don't have or know any other way of letting it out."

These acts of self-punishment are not working. You are continuing the acts of the perpetrators in your life by becoming one—only toward yourself. You do have a great need for counseling in order to explore how to grieve the past abuse and how to stop abusing yourself.

You can no longer bury these wounds. Unexpressed grief will come out in unhealthy and destructive ways. When anger is not expressed assertively, it turns into depression or aggression. My opinion is that your anger has turned into both. And when depression is not treated it increases. It does not go away.

We are made with a grief mechanism. As humans we need to feel the pain inside—the anger, sadness, disappointment, loneliness, etc. It is healthy to feel the emotions and then express them to others. We need to be heard and validated.

You also need to work through the victimization you have experienced. When one is abused, the psyche is affected, and you will feel a loss of control and a great sense of helplessness.

When you feel like a victim, you will try to gain control in any way you can—even when your behavior becomes unhealthy or ineffective.

As you can see, you have many issues to work through. I would challenge your statement, "I don't think I am far-gone enough to see one [a counselor]." This sounds like denial and minimization of your issues. How much further will you journey into depression and self-mutilation before you get help?

You need intervention now. There are community mental health services available that provide a sliding scale for counseling. Take advantage of this. Also, many health care plans include mental health coverage for counseling. I suspect that you will need to consider medication for your depression. See your family doctor for an evaluation. Many times churches have counseling centers or the pastor will meet and pray with you. Consider all the resources available including books, articles, etc. You need to discover how to rebuild your self worth. Read the book The Search for Significance by Robert McGee. May God bless you as you decide to make changes in your life and get the help you need to recover from your abusive past and present.

Question — Abused as a child and now I abuse: I grew up in a very violent atmosphere and I was beaten throughout most of my life. Before I would just take it and then go on with my business, but when I reached about the age of 16 I became very defensive and violent towards anyone who would attack me. For example, one time my dad got mad at me and grabbed me by the back of the neck, and before I could even think about it, I punched him in the face. It seems like I have gone through such a violent childhood that whenever someone gets aggressive towards me and then grabs or pushes me, before I can even think about it I lash out! A couple of times my fiancée has pushed me when she was mad about something, and both times that has happened something in my head flashed a big red STOP sign before I even came close to lashing out. I love her more than anything, and I trust that because of that I would never hurt her! I am asking for help because even though I think that, I have to be 100 percent positive that I won't do anything! Please let me know what you think or a way you could help.

Answer — You need to have a plan to prevent your anger from escalating. Once anger is triggered your flight/flight response is triggered in less than one second. Thus you don't have much of a chance to stop a harmful reaction, and with your background you might hurt the one you love.

It sounds like neither of you has skills to talk through conflict in a healthy way. When either of you notices tension or conflict in the relationship—hurt or misunderstanding—call a time-out for at least thirty minutes.

During the time-out ask: what am I angry or frustrated about? What is the issue? What do I need or want to happen? How can I communicate my need with compassion? How will my request benefit the relationship and meet my fiancée's needs? Then come back ready to listen as well as to communicate your needs respectfully.

Review the time-out, assertiveness and conflict management chapters for more help in changing the way you respond to triggers which provoke you to anger.

If you seek counsel with a professional, ask if he or she has been trained in anger management. See www.aacc.net for a directory of counselors.

Question — Mentally abusive spouse: I am married to a man who I believe mentally abuses me. I am confused and depressed. I do not know how to deal with this. I am tired and have no energy most of the time. Where do I start to fix this?

Answer — You are not alone. Many women are suffering in marriages such as yours. You need to learn how to cope and how to take better care of yourself through building your self-esteem, seeking spiritual guidance, developing assertiveness skills, and getting some support.

Please call the National Domestic Violence hotline at 1-800-799-7233 or contact www.aacc.net for a referral to a mental health professional. You need to get some counseling and resources.

Go to your family doctor or a psychiatrist for an evaluation about your depression. You need a complete physical exam to find out if your hormones and thyroid are functioning normally since there may be a physiological basis for your depression besides this stressful situation. When people experience an ongoing crisis or stress or conflict they can suffer depression, and this depletes the neurochemicals in the brain that affect their mood.

Your husband needs an anger management or a batterer's intervention program. Ask your husband to attend counseling with you or a marriage retreat. Read the book Fighting for Your Marriage by Scott Stanley and Howard Markman. This book will teach both of you healthy communication and problem-solving skills.

You need to develop and apply assertiveness skills as taught in this book. Take a time-out when your husband becomes verbally abusive. Let him know prior to a conflict that you will be implementing this technique to give both of you a break to cool-down and consider what the issues are. After the time-out period (thirty minutes to an hour) you can talk with him about the issue as you see it and make some requests. Make sure you talk about the problem within twenty-four hours. If he follows you around the house verbally abusing you, you should leave the house until he can calm down. If he threatens you—in any way—you will need to call the police and possibly find a safe place to stay.

The reason that you feel so confused, depressed, and fatigued is that you feel helpless and hopeless about your marriage and the emotional pain you feel when he is verbally abusing you. Assertiveness, counseling, faith, friends who are supportive, pastoral guidance and medication (if needed) can help you improve your situation and life.

Take care of yourself. Get some exercise. Think about going back to school or getting a part-time job. Take some time to get together with friends.

Many times verbal and mental abuse will escalate. You need to be prepared with a safety plan. In this case, you need to seek domestic violence resources.

Question — Annoyed at myself for lashing out: I'm sorry if this is a little disjointed and confusing. I'm pretty sure I'm just whining. I haven't been through half the things everyone else seems to have, but there's just something in my head that I can't seem to get a handle on. I'm pretty annoyed at myself that I hit someone. He got on me about a few little things, and I just turned around and belted him. This is not just boys fighting—I'm female for a start—he's twice my size and twice my age. The more you tell him something, the more he yells. It's like a case of "I'm big, your little, I'm right, you're wrong. End of story." Everyone else seems to be able to just get over it. I seem to just fester in it. I can't channel it anywhere, I can't untangle it, and I can't get rid of it. What else can I do? What if the next person is someone who actually matters—my boyfriend, or my mom, or some little kid?

Answer — Why not get some anger management counseling since you seem to fly off the handle so quickly? You need to explore what is happening—what the triggers are and how to apply some coping skills.

Your flight/flight mechanism is easily irritated so you need to recognize and control your anger early on. Taking a time-out when you feel tension in your neck or your stomach will give you an opportunity to think about what the issue is and what possible steps to take.

I wonder what you are telling yourself when you get angry? Maybe you are dealing with some catastrophic, all or nothing thinking. Or maybe you are personalizing, and mind-reading. Distorted thinking will contribute greatly to the escalation of anger.

Your friend has a big problem with anger as well. Both of you would benefit from anger management classes or intervention.

You can begin to apply the skills taught in this book. And concentrate on stress management so that you can learn to relax and change any hot self-talk to more soothing self-talk.

Question — I blow-up so fast: When I get angry, I blow up so fast that I don't have time to stop and think or ask for God's wisdom. I know all of these things would help, but by the time I think of it I've already done the damage. What can I do to help get control of my temper?

Answer — Anger is provoked by a combination of sources: low self-worth, recurring patterns, disappointments, revenge, depression, sin and/or selfishness, lack of skills, too much stress, physical, emotional or relationship problems.

Some people hold their anger inside and then blow up at a small trigger later on. I recommend taking the following steps:

Write out and log recent times of anger. Explore what happened, what the issue was, how you felt, and what resulted. Then think of times in the past when you were able to control your anger. What did you do or say? What did you tell yourself that calmed you down?

Learn to take "time-outs" immediately. You can walk away from situations/people that trigger your anger. Give yourself time to cool off. Take a run, pray, and think. What is the real issue and what are the feelings underlying your anger? What do you want to request from the person? How can you negotiate some conflict you are having?

Avoid lots of caffeine. Completely avoid alcohol and drugs (unless you are taking a prescription). Caffeine increases your metabolism, heart rate, and blood pressure and causes mood irritability. Alcohol and drugs may give a person a "high" or mellow feeling at first and seem to relieve stress, but the effects are temporary. Soon afterwards you will actually feel more irritable and depressed, and angry feelings will usually escalate.

Assess your stress: You may be dealing with a lot of stress or loss. This needs to be explored and worked through, possibly with the help of a counselor. Explore how you can decrease stress in your life. Begin an exercise program so you can work off some of the stress in your life physically.

Learn to communicate assertively. This is one of the most important tools for expressing your anger in a healthy way. Begin to share your needs, requests and opinions more openly and lovingly. Start setting boundaries to avoid taking on responsibilities which rightfully belong to others.

Depression can play a part in anger or vice versa. I would encourage you to go to counseling and see a psychiatrist for a diagnosis and the appropriate medication. You can contact www.aacc.net for a referral to a counselor and psychiatrist in your area.

Question — Struggling with intense anger as a Christian: I am a believer in Christ. I grew up in an abusive home and was rejected and made fun of by my peers at school. Now, years later, I am still working on my self-worth. I know who I am in Christ, on a mental level, but I still wrestle about being a doormat and nonassertive. My problem, believe it or not, is I am struggling with intense anger and frustration about a co-worker who is a fellow believer but acts "holier than thou" and elitist. She is very condescending to me. She knows my weakness and plays me. I know I need to learn to stand

159

up, so I have begun on working on assertiveness. She talked down to me in the office last Friday, in front of everyone, about something I was innocent of. It was the final straw. I need to get a grip on this and do what God would have me do. She would be shocked if I told her I do not consider her a friend. But, I have come to realize she is not, if she treats me like I am inferior to her. I feel discriminated against. What should I do?

Answer — You have a right to be angry and to work through the anger in a healthy way. Here are some suggestions. It's very difficult working with someone like you describe who won't take responsibility for her actions and behavior and at the same time professes to be a Christian.

The most important step for you is to grow in assertiveness (speaking the truth in love) and to be able to forgive. I suggest you confront that woman with the fact that you felt humiliated when she said unkind words in front of the group at work (use the exact words she said that were disrespectful, but don't accuse her of being disrespectful).

Request that she come to you in private whenever she has a problem with you or your work in the future so you can discuss it one-on-one rather than bringing it up in front of a group. Tell her that coming to you privately will help improve your relationship and communication.

If she continues to put you down in a group, then you may need to ask your supervisor to mediate this issue between the two of you. No matter what happens, you need to be ready with an appropriate response if this co-worker makes derogatory or accusatory remarks about you in front of a group. Interrupt her by saying, "Excuse me. I think that it would be good for you to speak with me in private about this matter. I suggest we go to the coffee room or my office to discuss it."

You can also write out what usually happens so you are prepared for the next time she says something hurtful about you in a group. You may even have to say, "What you just said was really hurtful and I disagree with you" in front of everyone. Saying this should be a last-resort response but will express your real feelings and the fact that her behavior is inappropriate.

The Bible says, "The tongue has the power of life and death," and "The tongue that brings healing is a tree of life, but a deceitful tongue crushes the spirit." It also tells us to "speak the truth in love" and "Do not let any unwholesome talk come out of your mouths, but only what is helpful for building others up according to their needs, that it may benefit those who listen."[1]

Question — How can I tell when my anger is getting out of control?

Answer — Simply stated, you can tell you have a problem with anger when it is:

- too frequent,

- too intense,

- lasts too long,

- leads to aggression,

- disturbs work or relationships,

- causes you to feel resentful towards and distant from others.

Question — Can someone or something cause me to get angry?

Answer — Someone or something can seem to make us angry, but events and people only have the power to tempt us to become angry. We make the choice to get angry and the choice about how to respond. At first we may blame the person or situation for our anger, but in reality we choose to be angry based on the beliefs we hold about a particular event.

Remember, that anger can be righteous and good. When someone disrespects or harms you—you will feel angry and need to respond assertively. When someone steals your purse or wallet—you will feel angry and need to call the police and file charges against him/her. When someone hits your child you will feel angry and need to call DCFS or the police. When someone is just out to "get your goat" by treating you with sarcasm and "put-downs"—you will feel angry and need to walk away. You don't need to listen or let them continue to mistreat you.

Anger is a choice based on perception and the situation. You can choose to get angry when ruminating over an event or person, without anything occurring to provoke you. You choose anger. "Anyone who angers you controls you" wrote Sister Kenny. You let that person control your negative feelings.

Question — Self-mutilation: Yesterday I tortured myself again. No offense to you, but my family isn't religious. In fact I haven't been to church since I was five. I do agree with you about getting help, but it's too hard right now. I do not think I can just stop after all these years of doing it and keeping it a secret. I really don't know what to do. I am afraid to be alone and yet I want to be alone. I will be 16 this October and I have done this sort of stuff since I was nine years old, I think. To tell you the truth, I don't even remember when I started—it was so long ago. I need help now! But I don't know how to get it.

Answer — Most teens who self-mutilate say they are angry and hold their feelings in. One teen puts it this way: "I don't cry because I cut—I cut because I cry!"

You are probably very angry, lonely, depressed, stressed, punishing yourself, fearful, sad, and needing to express those feelings. Many people say they get a "high" from self-injury. That "high" quickly dissolves into feelings of guilt, self-loathing, more depression, anger and a sense of failure.

You need to tell someone. Maybe your parents are not the ones to tell, but you must find an adult you can trust and can talk to. You also need counseling and a physical exam.

Why not commit to doing three things before you begin to self-mutilate?

1. *Pray.* You need a Higher Power to help you. You may not be religious, but anyone can talk to God. Even the Twelve Steps of Alcoholics Anonymous teach people that they must begin to admit they can't manage their addiction alone — that they need to turn to a Higher Power for help.

2. *Express yourself.* Write out what you are feeling. What is the pain? What is the anger about? Are you taking out on yourself the anger you feel towards someone else? What disappointment just occurred that triggers feelings of helplessness and hopelessness about life? Call a friend, aunt or uncle and talk about what is going on in your life. You don't have to start by admitting that you have a problem with self-harm. You can just talk about what issues are disturbing you — whether it's your parents or school or feeling bad about your life.

3. *Do something productive.* Go for a walk or ride your bike. You need to exercise and think over the issues which are troubling you Begin a hobby such as photography. You need "something to do" which will build your self-esteem and give you something to look forward to.

I am challenging you to start doing something. Only you can decide to change. You can decide whether or not you want God's help. No one can make you change. You are suffering inside and need comfort, hope, and power to stop mutilating yourself. Move on to a better life—the one that God planned for you. Consider reading The Purpose-Driven Life by Rick Warren or An Anchor for the Soul: Help for the Present, Hope for the Future by Ray Pritchard.

Question — Problem with rage: I have a rage problem. It begins with a jealousy problem and turns into out-of-control rage where I want to throw things, curse, cry, yell, and push or hit. My mouth gets out of control and soon I am in tears and break something. This has led to fights and separations I do not want, but I feel insecure that my body is not as pretty as another woman's and that my boyfriend might compare hers to mine and not like mine anymore. It is the Jealousy Rage I cannot control! I want to honor God but cannot stop thinking these things constantly, daily. I have prayed, but when the emotions come, I do not know how to handle them!

Answer — Certainly your rage and jealousy are out of control. What is the real problem underlying your rage and anger? And what can you do about your problem? I suggest that your problem is not the man you are with or the other women with whom you compete or even a preoccupation about your appearance and your sexuality. You are looking to find yourself—you are searching for significance and security. You are really trying to convince yourself that you are a person of value and worth. Since you are not convinced, you are hoping that a man's attraction and attention will cause you to feel better about who you are.

There's a problem with what you are doing. It's not working. The men you are dating can't give you enough attention, and if they did you would find their attention deficient no matter what. The only one who can convince you that you are a valuable person is you!

What will it matter ten years from now whether someone is prettier or sexier than you? Especially if in your jealousy and rage you have driven away the people who are the most important in your life. The real question is what are you living for? Right now the focus is all about you. Yes, it may be due to your insecurities and some brokenness in your past, but you can change. You see, when a person is so focused on getting their needs met they become self-absorbed. Whatever need you have underneath the anger and jealousy becomes the center of your life.

Give up the anger—give up the rage. Ask God for His help and forgiveness. Read the First Edition of What's Good About Anger? to find out more about how faith can help defuse your anger and meet your needs. You may very well benefit from professional counseling because you are manifesting signs of depression and paranoia along with low self-esteem, rage, and obsessions.

God bless you in your journey to find freedom from the bondage of rage and jealousy and to discover a whole new life!

Question — Can't get angry: I cannot get angry. Last week someone stole $40.00 from me, and I didn't even care. I always get into situations that should make me burst, but I don't. I am never angry. That might seem good, but it's terrible. I can't show any anger or anything like that. Can I have some advice on getting angry and staying angry?

Answer — It seems like you have shut down your feelings. You know in your mind that you have a right to be angry, but your emotions are paralyzed. Maybe this is how you react to anything that should emit a negative emotion such as fear, frustration, irritation, hopelessness, loneliness, anger. Maybe your positive feelings are shut-down as well.

In the past you may have learned that it was wrong to be angry or perhaps any reaction you had was ignored or disregarded by your parents. You learned to stuff down your feelings in childhood and thus you still hold in your emotions now.

My question is: what did you tell yourself when the person stole money from you last week?

1. "It's only money. I can get more. So what." (You minimized the loss.)

2. "Maybe the guy needed the money more than me." (An overly codependent response demonstrating low self-esteem.)

3. "Oh well ... just another bad thing that happened to me. I can't worry about this." (Hopeless talk.)

Maybe you rationalize anger and call it stress, disappointment, fear, irritability.

I suggest you write out what happened to you. Ask yourself: what are the losses I experienced because this guy stole money from me? Maybe you could not afford to pay a bill or get a special gift for your wife, etc. What will you have to do to recoup the money and pay the bill or buy the gift? Are you feeling a twinge of tension in your neck or a knot in your stomach? Do you hear yourself saying, "That was wrong. How unfair that I was violated! That guy should repay me!"

If you feel any of those physiological reactions and hear yourself saying any of these things, you are angry! Step out on your anger. Take the energy it brings to you and try to do something about the situation. For example, report the theft to the police. If you know the person who stole it, ask for the money back and tell him/her that you will report it to the police if it is not returned. If you don't do something, this person will continue to steal and may even steal again from you. Use the energy you get from anger to resolve the issues that come up in your life in assertive and healthy ways. Continuing to give-up or deny the situations which should make you angry will only lead to feelings of helplessness, victimization, depression and distrust.

Question — Spouse will not forgive: My spouse will not forgive me for the hurtful words I spouted during an argument. She says she cannot forgive me. I am waiting patiently for her to give our marriage another start, but she says she won't change her mind. What can I do?

Answer — Once you have apologized—wait it out. Don't pressure her. You want her to willingly forgive and freely love you. You can only change yourself. Most likely, she will forgive eventually and will give the marriage another try.

Angry outbursts bring consequences. It's important to figure out where your anger is coming from and how to deal with the root cause. The underlying issue usually has to do with fear or catastrophic thinking. When we feel fearful, we respond by trying to control others. Controlling behaviors generally create a negative reaction from those around us. No one wants to be controlled. Controlling anger pushes the people we are trying to control away. And we don't get what we want—relationship and respect.

Work on yourself and your growth in managing anger. When your wife sees that she can trust you because you are changing—she may forgive and give you a second chance.

Appendix: Inventories for Empathy and Assertiveness

The following inventory is designed for personal use and for discussion. Check the characteristics and tendencies which best describe you thoughtfully and honestly. Do not score or read the instructions for scoring until you have completed the inventory. Complete any examples required as instructed on the scoring page.

Empathy Inventory © copyright 2021 by Lynette J. Hoy, NCC, LCPC
(may not be duplicated in any form)

1. When I am talking with someone—I find it hard to listen: ___

2. When someone is speaking—I generally am thinking about what I want to say and miss what they have said: ___

3. When someone is speaking—I usually ask clarifying questions so I can understand what they have said: ___
   (check if you go back later with clarifying questions)

4. When others are talking—I try to paraphrase or summarize what they said: ___

5. When someone is talking about a problem—I try to pick up on their feelings and say, "you seem stressed out by work or disappointed with your life": ___

6. Others have told me I am a good listener: ___

7. People come to me when they have problems for encouragement: ___

8. I try to see things from other people's point of view even when I disagree with them: ___

9. I try to impress on others the point I want to get across: ___

10. I turn conversations around or change the topic so I can say what I believe is really important: ___

11. I have difficulty identifying feelings and emotions in myself: ___

12. I have difficulty identifying feelings and emotions in others: ___

13. When someone seems troubled—I generally ask them what is happening: ___

14. When someone doesn't share my opinion—I either explain myself in greater detail or stop talking to the person: ___

15. I can easily identify strengths and weaknesses in my life: ___

16. When someone shares a problem and their feelings—I explore what may be the cause with them: ___

17. When my goals are in contrast to others—I usually try to negotiate with those in disagreement: ___

18. Most people say that I am a caring, thoughtful person: ___

19. People complain that I am "self-centered": ___

20. Significant people in my life say that I am driven to achieve my goals: ___

21. Some people say that I'm a poor listener: ___

22. People say that I am able to manage my anger and emotions: ___

23. I don't find it necessary to pressure people into believing the way I do about something important to me: ___

24. I try to imagine what it's like to be in someone else's situation and what they might be experiencing: ___

25. When someone is angry or frustrated with me—I have a hard time listening to their complaint or remarks: ___

© *copyright 2021 by Lynette J. Hoy, NCC, LCPC*

Score the Empathy inventory:

A. Numbers 1, 2, 9, 10, 11, 12, 14, 19, 20, 21, 25 = 0 (zero).

B. Add 1 point each for numbers: 3, 4, 5, 6, 7, 8, 13, 15, 16, 17, 18, 22, 23, 24. (provide recent examples for each one of the B category statements on another sheet)

Empathy rating: 0 = Heartless; 2-4 = Low; 5 = Half-hearted; 6-10 = Moderate; 11-13 = High; 14 = Bleeding Heart

Assertiveness Inventory

This inventory will help you determine whether you are appropriately assertive, i.e., respectfully honest and direct about your feelings and opinions with others. Check the statements only if these are generally true of you. Be honest.

When expressing myself, I generally:

1. ___ have difficulty being clear and direct.

2. ___ keep quiet letting others speak.

3. ___ am abrasive or demanding.

4. ___ leave wishing I had said more.

5. ___ become too loud.

6. ___ say too much.

7. ___ clearly state how I feel or what I think.

8. ___ use active listening, tact and respect.

9. ___ ask others for their opinions after stating mine.

10. ___ tend to manipulate.

11. ___ make indirect suggestions about my feelings and thoughts.

12. ___ state my thoughts without denigrating someone's character.

13. ___ clarify what other people say.

14. ___ base my opinion on facts and behavior.

15. ___ label or stereotype others.

16. ___ consider others' opinions as well as my own.

17. ___ find fault with other people.

18. ___ use a firm voice when necessary.

19. ___ use forceful gestures.

20. ___ communicate concern for others.

21. ___ quietly rationalize why I didn't speak up.

22. ___ hint about my feelings and wants.

23. ___ speak calmly and directly.

24. ___ turn conversations around to my needs and agenda.

25. ___ confront unpleasant issues directly but, with gentleness.

26. ___ when I am angry—I tend to shut-down and give the "cold shoulder."

27. ___ when I am frustrated—I don't hold back any of my feelings.

28. ___ I have difficulty communicating my ideas to others.

Once you have finished this inventory go to the scoring page to rate yourself.

Rate yourself as:

1. Appropriately assertive if you checked most of these: 7, 8, 9, 12, 13, 14, 16, 18, 20, 23, 25.

2. Passively pining if you checked any of these: 1, 2, 4, 21, 26, 28

3. Mostly manipulative if you checked: 10, 11, 22, 24

4. Aggressive, overbearing or blaming if you checked: 3, 5, 6, 15, 17, 19, 27

5. Muddled mess: you use various tactics mixed with assertiveness if you checked some statements from more than one of the categories.

NOTES

This edition provides several references or paraphrases from the Holy Bible for greater insights and examples into anger and healthy responses to it.

Chapter Three:
1. Ephesians 4:25
2. Romans 12:19

Chapter Four:
1. James 1:19
2. Proverbs 22:24
3. Proverbs 15:1

Chapter Six:
1. Nehemiah 5:6-7
2. James 1:19

Chapter Eight:
1. Colossians 3:12-14
2. I Corinthians 13:4-5

Chapter Nine:
1. Ephesians 4:32

Chapter Thirteen:
1. Philippians 4:8

FAQ's:
1. Proverbs 18:21; 15:4;
   Ephesians 4:15, 29.

BIBLIOGRAPHY

Ali, Dr. Amir. The Article Collection of M. Amir Ali, Ph.D. "Forgiveness." Date of access: February 2, 2006.

<http://www.ilaam.net/Forgiveness.html> *a personal website.*

Backus, William. *Hidden Rift With God*. Minneapolis, MN: Bethany House, 1990.

Burns, D. *Feeling Good*. New York: Signet, 1980.

Carlson, Dwight L., M.D. *Overcoming Hurts & Anger*. Eugene, OR: Harvest House, 1981.

Dobson, Dr. James and Dobson, Shirley. *Night Light: A Devotional for Couples*. Sisters, OR: Multnomah, Inc., 2000.

Feindler, E.L. and Ecton, R.B. *Adolescent Anger Control: Cognitive-Behavioral Techniques*. New York: Pergamon Press, 1986.

Gintner, Dr. Gary. *Behavioral Anger Reduction Kit (BARK)*. Louisiana State University, 1995. Used by permission. E-mail: gintner@lsu.edu. Our thanks to Dr. Gintner for the use of his manual's statistics, anger triggers, the process of anger and thinking ahead reminders.

Goleman, Daniel. *Working with Emotional Intelligence*. New York: Bantam Books, 2000.

Hauck, Dr. Paul A. *Overcoming Frustration and Anger*. Westminster John Knox Press; Dimensions, 1974.

Holmes, T.H. and Rahe, R.H. "The Social Readjustment Rating Scale." Journal of Psychosomatic Research, 11:213-218, 1967.

McKay, M., Rogers, P.D. and McKay, J. *When Anger Hurts: Quieting the Storm Within*. Oakland: New Harbinger, 1989.

Potter-Efron, Ron. *Rage, A Step-by-Step Guide to Overcoming Explosive Anger*. Oakland, CA: New Harbinger Publication, Inc, 2007.

Potter-Efron, Ron. *Healing the Angry Brain*. Oakland, CA: New Harbinger Publication, Inc, 2012.

Prager, Dennis. "Response." The Sunflower. New York: Schocken Books, 1998. 225-30.

Pran, Dith. "Response." The Sunflower. New York: Schocken Books, 1998. 230-3.

Ricard, Matthieu. "Response." The Sunflower. New York: Schocken Books. 1998. 235-6.

Yancey, Philip. "An Unnatural Act." Christianity Today. 8 April 1991: 36-39.

ABOUT THE AUTHORS

Lynette J. Hoy is a Licensed Clinical Professional Counselor in the state of Illinois, a National Certified Counselor and a credentialed Anger Management Specialist-V, D i p l o m a t e , Supervisor and Consultant with the National Anger Management Association. Mrs. Hoy is also a Board Certified Professional Christian Counselor, a crisis counselor and domestic violence advocate. Lynette has counseled and trained hundreds of clients, couples, and students in anger management. She has trained and certified hundreds of counselors, professionals, and leaders in anger management. Lynette presents various classes, workshops, and marriage seminars. She and her husband David have been married over fifty-one years and have one married daughter. Lynette's experience of growing up in an abusive home and then counseling clients struggling with anger has provided the motivation for writing the What's Good About Anger? books, various anger management articles, workbooks, and training manuals. Lynette's faith in God gave her a foundation for loving and forgiving her father.

Ted Griffin worked as Senior Editor of Crossway Books, a division of Good News Publishers, for thirty years and is currently retired. He has authored numerous gospel tracts, including the best-selling You're Special, and is working on several books. He is a mentor, small group facilitator, and adult Sunday school teacher. He and his wife, Lois (deceased), were married over 45 years and have two grown children and five grandchildren. Having grown up under an alcoholic father, he has personally struggled with and has extensively studied anger issues.

Anyone desiring to contact the authors by e-mail is invited to do so:

Lynette Hoy: lynettehoy@gmail.com

Ted Griffin: twordsmith@aol.com

Anger Management Institute
Resources and Programs
by

Lynette Hoy and Ted Griffin

1. What's Good About Anger? Biblical Keys for Transforming Anger—for Christians and those seeking a faith-based approach to anger, 2014. Lynette Hoy and Ted Griffin.

2. Keys to Resolving Anger, Conflict, & Resentment in Marriage, 2017. Lynette Hoy and Seigel Bartley.

3. What's Good About Anger? Expanded 16-lesson combination book/workbooks for Adults, Teens, Couples and Kids.

What's Good
About Anger?
Workbook for Kids

Keys to Resolving
Anger, Conflict, &
Resentment in Marriage

4. Anger management certificate courses for individuals needing personal growth or who are required to fulfill court or employer orders for anger management. Online, 6-52 weeks/hours.

5. Anger Management Trainer-Specialist Certification Courses (Online/home-study) and live Workshops/Webinars for counselors, law enforcement or probation officers, educators, professionals, pastors, lay leaders and group facilitators. Adult and adolescent curriculum, assessment tools, power point presentation, DVDs, leader's guides.

6. What's Good About Anger? DVD with Lynette Hoy and Steve Yeschek, Anger Management Specialists.

Visit the Anger Management Institute site for resources at www.whatsgoodaboutanger.com and www.copingwithanger.com. Contact Lynette Hoy at 630.368.1880, or lynettehoy@gmail.com.